Mother Cub

Mother Cub

✦

One Woman's Journey to Save Her Son

Susan Lynn Perry

Best-selling author of Procrastination Elimination

iUniverse, Inc.

New York Lincoln Shanghai

Mother Cub
One Woman's Journey to Save Her Son

Copyright © 2007 by Susan Lynn Perry

iUniverse books may be ordered through booksellers or by contacting:

iUniverse
2021 Pine Lake Road, Suite 100
Lincoln, NE 68512
www.iuniverse.com
1-800-Authors (1-800-288-4677)

ISBN: 978-0-595-47918-4 (pbk)
ISBN: 978-0-595-60052-6 (ebk)

Printed in the United States of America

Contents

Preface

This is a book about courage, determination, and the willingness to take responsibility about a child's health. In ***Mother Cub: One Woman's Journey to Save Her Son***, Susan Lynn Perry shares with us the travails of single motherhood with the extra challenge of dealing with a son who is always sick and experiencing unexplainable behavioral difficulties.

Children do not come with an 'owner's manual' when they are born. New mothers depend on their own mothers, their peers, available literature, and the help of their medical professionals to help nurture and provide their children with the best care in the first years of their lives. Justin's health challenges tested his mother's mettle. Her love and determination to question the "system" pushed her to find an alternative option which has proved to put Justin on the path to being a normal little boy.

This book provides hope and the resources to help any parent with a child who is given the diagnosis of autism. It also shows that when something does not feel right, we should follow our instincts and find out why.

Lorna L. Engleman, MD
Lifestyle and Wellness Personal Coach
lorna@lornaenglemanmd.com
www.lornaenglemanmd.com
www.healthylifestylesa.com

Introduction

"Your son is having "some issues"."
"Your son seems to have a slight delay."
"Your son is displaying some autistic behaviors."
"Your son is definitely on the spectrum."
"Your son has PDD-NOS."
"Your son has Autism."

And then there's my all-time favorite.... "Your son is perfectly fine. He's just developing a little slower than most."

That last one came from my son's pediatrician. Let me re-phrase that. It was from my son's *former* pediatrician. After listening to that doctor for over a year and delaying doing anything about my son's condition, I finally got up the courage to get a second opinion. And then a third. And then a fourth.

All of the sentences listed above were used to define my son, Justin, between his first and fourth years of life, but none of them were delivered to me with a resounding finality that I could accept as the cold, hard truth. And every time I asked for clarification or tried to question the "professional" in order to try and figure out what the heck was going on, I was typically waved off as an overprotective, hypochondriac, hysterical mother.

Sound familiar? I'm willing to bet that you or someone you know has experienced some of the same treatment.

What does it all mean? I often wondered during that hectic, confusing time. *And, why are they all telling me something different?* What I didn't know at the time (but would soon come to learn) was that they were all saying the *same* thing. They simply each had a slightly different way of saying it.

How could my son have autism? And why did I waste an entire year listening to his doctor say "nothing's wrong"—when I could have been doing something about it? Aren't we supposed to be able to rely on our doctor's opinion?

I was angry, confused, hurt and scared, but I decided that none of those things would help my son. I decided the best thing I could do for Justin would be to learn everything I could about autism and how to deal with it. So I went to the Internet and quickly found out little is really known about this confusing and complicated condition. There's a lot of information out there on the web, but a lot of it is contradictory.

As I weeded through the confusion of solid, well-founded research versus conspiracy theory rhetoric, I became educated about autism, the symptoms, the causes, and the treatments. And there was one thing that kept coming up over and over again. *There is no cure for autism.*

No cure. The words reverberated around in my brain for days as I tried to wrap my mind around the fact that my little boy would never have a normal life. My husband and family tried their best to console me, but I felt like I had been handed a death sentence.

I was disappointed to find out exactly how little is taught in medical school about autism. It's also disturbing that such an extreme diagnosis is often given with very little standardized and/or medical testing to back it up. I was dismayed that Justin's doctor would tell me there's nothing wrong with my son at the same time that other professionals were telling me that he had such a serious condition.

Luckily, I started listening to my instincts instead of the doctor. Luckily, I took the time and effort to find out the truth about my son's condition. Luckily, I was able to find out that Justin does not have a genetic "there's no cure" form of autism, at all. What Justin is suffering from is heavy metal toxicity. Research shows the symptoms of each are often one and the same.

I was horrified to learn that Justin's first vaccination contained over 43 times the level of mercury in it that the EPA considers safe. It was full of a preservative called Thimerosal, which is 50% mercury by weight. Justin was nineteen days old and only six pounds. Several of the vaccinations he received after that also contained mercury, and with each subsequent dose, he became more and more sick.

The mercury ingredient is added in some vaccinations so the pharmaceutical companies can get a longer shelf life out of each vial. The vaccination solution is protected and preserved for longer use, but our kids are then damaged for the rest of their lives. The pharmaceutical companies have known about the dangers of mercury for decades, yet to date there has still been no worldwide ban on the use of it in shots that our children continue to receive every day.

This is "big stuff" in the media right now with lots of so-called experts saying there is no Thimerosal in childhood vaccinations anymore. What they are often downplaying, however, is the horrendous amount of damage that's been done to an entire generation of kids. Don't be fooled into thinking you and your children have escaped any harm either. Thimerosal (i.e. mercury) is still used today in many influenza and tetanus vaccinations.

According to Dr. Russell Blaylock as printed in the Blaylock Wellness Report, "Mercury is listed as one of the top six most poisonous metals on earth. Numerous studies have shown that even very low doses can alter how the brain functions—especially in terms of memory, concentration, motor control and behavior."[1]

I was mortified to learn about what had been injected into my son's body. Mortified, but strangely excited too, because I quickly found out that mercury poisoning can be treated. It's not easy, but it can be done. And now, through the diligent application of biomedical treatments, I'm happy to say that my son has been able to make tremendous gains in a very short amount of time.

Thanks to interventions such as nutritional supplements, a gluten-free casein-free diet, speech therapy and heavy metal detoxification, I've been able to experience the joy of my son's language exploding from a typical two-word sentence of "That one" to "Mommy, the computer's not working", and "I'm having strawberries with my dinner." And all of this has happened in less than five months' time.

Just think—if I had not had the guts to question his doctor, my son probably would have regressed to the point of no language at all by this time.

Who am I? I am a hard-working, concerned, loving, worried parent of a very bright, delightful little boy named Justin. And this is my story of how I went about getting to the bottom of my son's health issues. This is about how I followed my instincts and ultimately saved my son from retreating completely into the isolated world of autism.

I decided to write this book to share with other parents who are going through or will soon be going through what I did. This is not intended to be medical advice at all. It is simply my story of how I went about discovering the truth and how—with a little luck, a lot of support and unwavering determination—I was able to help him get better.

I hope and pray you're able to do the same for your precious child … or grandchild … or nephew.… .

If you take nothing else away from my story, please take this one piece of advice. Be a mother cub. Follow your instincts when it comes to your child. You know him/her better than anyone else, and it's your job to do everything you can to make the world a better place for your little one. If you have even the slightest nagging suspicion that something might be wrong with your child, be diligent and ask questions until you find out for sure.

Before I go on, I need to say one thing. I would highly advise you to consult your child's medical practitioner before trying anything mentioned in this book. Every child is different and each will respond differently to treatment, supplementation, therapy and nutrition. This is simply my story of what has worked for my son.

Autism symptoms are very complex. In fact, they are so complex that the medical and educational communities refer to the condition as an "autism spectrum disorder" or ASD. ASD can include gastro-intestinal dysfunction, neurological issues, lack of social skills, impaired immune function, diminished nutrient uptake, along with behavioral problems. One problem often leads to another and then another. The multiple health problems that subsequently arise within your child help doctors and school officials determine that your child is "on the spectrum".

So the bottom line is—it's up to YOU to do your homework. Take the time to do your own research and find out the root cause of your child's symptoms. And once you do that, attack it aggressively and don't take no for an answer until your child is healthy again. I can promise you that each small step you take today will pay off in huge rewards tomorrow.

Most doctors will tell you that for autism—there is no cure. I'm not so sure about that. I think that's a defeatist attitude and one designed to encourage you to be dependent on the medical community. The reality is that autistic behaviors are difficult and expensive to treat, but they can be treated in ways other than to medicate your child with yet another pharmaceutical prescription like Ritalin or Risperdal.

It's crazy when you realize that pharmaceutical companies are manufacturing vaccinations for our children to "protect" them from measles, mumps, hepatitis, etc., but often damaging them in such a way that many develop life-long, chronic, auto-immune disorders which then require them to be dependent on other medications from the pharmaceutical companies. It's a hell-of-a racket for the pharmaceutical big boys.

But what about all of these damaged kids? And what about the parents struggling to take care of them? Who's looking out for us?

I've written this book in order to help other parents learn from my trial and error. You'll find in this book my actual journal entries from the first four years of my son's life. This is intended to inform, educate and inspire you. I want you to know that you *can* help your children get better. You just need to take one step …and then another …and then another.

For those of you wondering what the heck "Mother Cub" is supposed to mean, let me try and explain. When I was going through my seemingly endless research efforts and collecting all of my son's medical and vaccination records, there were a few unlucky individuals who received more than their fair share of my inquiries.

There was one man in particular who worked in the records department of one of my son's former doctors. For the sake of his privacy, we'll call him "Joe."

I never met "Joe" in person, but am assuming from his voice that he was an elderly man. One afternoon, I called for what was probably at least the fourth time that day. Every time I hung up the phone with him, I just kept coming up with more questions that needed answers.

After patiently waiting for me to finish my newest question regarding my son's records, he blurted out, "You know something, lady? You're worse than a Mother Cub!"

When I asked him what he meant, he said when a mother lion leaves her cubs to go in search of food, there is typically one cub in the litter that is more dominant than the others and tends to "fill in" for the mother lion while she's away. That cub is often referred to as the "mother cub" and tends to be fiercely loyal and protective of the other cubs.

Now, I don't know if there's any truth to that or not, but it stuck with me nevertheless. As a parent, I will always be fiercely loyal and protective of my little cub. I'm sure you feel the same way. (I think Joe was actually trying to say that I was being a real pain in his you-know-what, but I decided to take it as a compliment anyway.) ☺

Infancy

"A woman's love
Is mighty, but a mother's heart is weak,
And by its weakness overcomes."

—James Russell Lowell,

1

The Early Days

Justin started out just like most other little boys. My pregnancy was an easy one, and his delivery, though long and exhausting for me, was without any significant complications. His APGAR scores were close to perfect. He was happy, healthy, and on his way to developing into a remarkable little man. Little did I know back in March of 2003 how our worlds were about to change.

I have to say at this point that I am one of those true believers in the notion that there's a reason for everything. I now believe the reason I've been faced with the challenge of raising Justin is so I can tell my story to other parents and help educate and guide them along this difficult and confusing path.

Parenthood is hard enough, but throwing in a child with special needs really takes everything up a notch. There is never quite enough of you to go around. You've heard the adage, "It takes a village to raise a child," right? Well, when you're talking about a child with special needs, it's really more like, "It takes *being* a village to raise a child."

I was a fairly typical new mother. At least I think I was. I was overworked, underpaid, sleep-deprived and basically an emotional wreck. Perhaps that wasn't the experience you had. Maybe you juggled all of your new demands and still managed to be a cross between Cindy Crawford, Eva Longoria and June Cleaver.

I, on the other hand, was more like a cross between Kathy Griffin and Bridget Jones, which is actually what inspired me to write my book in this format. Although this book is about a very serious subject, and one obviously very close to my heart, I still manage to find a lot of humor in my daily life and I've tried to touch on some of that too.

My experience with early motherhood was pretty much a Molotov cocktail of raging hormones, an uncooperative body, very demanding job that didn't allow me much of a maternity leave, an unsupportive husband and a very cranky newborn. They don't write much about that kind of stuff in the mom-to-be magazines, do they?

I thought I was well-prepared for this thing called motherhood. In fact, I was pretty sure I might be the best-prepped Mom in the maternity ward. After all, I had read every book I could get my hands on, subscribed to every parenting magazine and spent hours and hours scouring the Internet, learning everything I could learn about my impending change in life.

But, as any veteran parent will tell you, nothing teaches quite like experience.

I breast-fed Justin for eight weeks, and then it was time for me to go back to work in the office. I managed a very busy engineering firm and knew that continuing to breastfeed was out of the question for me. So I reluctantly weaned my sweet son and started him on formula.

Unfortunately, Justin displayed an intolerance to regular formulas pretty early on, which resulted in a cranky, colicky baby a lot of the time. I chalked that up to a normal reaction of weaning from breast to bottle. I tried several different formulas and finally had to settle on a soy-based brand which seemed to suit him the best.

Even when I switched him to soy, however, he still had to sleep in his car seat which I placed in his crib every night. It allowed him to sleep on a slight incline, which helped in curbing some of the reflux, resulting in a slightly better night's sleep for all of us. His pediatrician didn't seem overly concerned, so neither were we.

As a lot of other parents out there, we were a two-income family, so Justin went to daycare during the day. This naturally meant that he picked up a lot of colds and ear infections from the other kids at daycare. But that's normal too, right?

It was rather challenging, to say the least, to juggle the demands of a full-time job, along with caring for an infant that was oftentimes too sick to go to daycare. But what did I know? Other parents were always lamenting about their children picking up germs from the daycare, so I accepted it as a slight inconvenience and didn't think much more of it.

In retrospect, I now know that it is not normal for your baby to be sick all of the time—even if he is in daycare. An occasional cold or ear infection, yes, but a weekly (almost daily) sickness is definitely not normal. Unless a baby's immune system has been compromised in some way, he or she should be able to handle most of the germs they come in contact with efficiently and expediently.

The following are journal entries from the early weeks. I'll apologize now for the random thoughts. (I was sort of all over the map in the early days.)

4/1/2003—We're home from the hospital. Yea!! Justin is so amazing—with his tiny little fingers and toes. The doctors say my little boy is perfect!! I'm so tired, but somehow seem to be running on major adrenaline. This is all so surreal. Maybe I can finally get some sleep now.

4/3/2003—The breast-feeding thing is not going so well. My boobs are so huge that Justin can't get his itty-bitty mouth latched on. I look ridiculously top-heavy. I don't know how Pamela Andersen does it. I constantly feel like if I stand up, I'll probably just fall over again. Best to stay laying down.

4/4/2003—God I'm tired.

4/6/2003—Big task for the day—take a shower!!

4/8/2003—I hurt all over. The doctor says I'm healing up great, but it feels like I've been hit by a two-ton truck. The breast-feeding thing is amazing now that Justin has finally figured it out.

4/12/2003—I have not had a full night's sleep in a really long, long time. Wasn't I just saying "now that I'm home, I can get some sleep"? What was I thinking? I walk around in this weird daze all day long and am amazed I can function at all. How do most people do this?

4/17/2003—Justin is nineteen days old and received his first vaccination today. It was awful!! He screamed and turned all red in the face, and I felt horribly guilty for subjecting him to that. I think it's strange that they give Hepatitis B shots to kids so little. I mean, isn't that a disease you get primarily through IV drug use and sexual contact with an infected party? How is a newborn baby at risk for that?

4/20/2003—Justin has had a runny nose for the last three days. Poor little guy. I think he may have inherited my allergies. Or maybe it's because of the shot the other day? Need to call the doctor.

4/21/2003—Called the doctor, who said it's probably just a little bug. Need to watch for worsening symptoms and bring in if it gets worse.

4/26/2003—I started working out again. Not a good idea. Ice cream and chocolate is a much better idea.

5/10/2003—It's getting harder for me to keep these notes. Best baby invention—bouncy seat. I strap Justin in there, turn it on and he just gets his little groove on and is very, very happy.

5/29/2003—We had a big round of shots today. 5 shots total, including Hepatitis B, DPT, Polio, HIB, and Pneumococcal. Seems like an awful lot to give to such a little guy at one time. Justin slept the whole way home and most of the day. He was pretty cranky for the entire evening. Why don't they space out the shots more? I don't see how that much stuff being injected all at once can be a good thing for someone so small.

5/30/2003—Justin slept a lot today. He doesn't seem to be feeling very well, and is kind of lethargic. I better get some sleep too, while I can.

6/3/2003—Started weaning Justin from breast-feeding and trying to find a formula that works for him. The poor little fella is not doing well with formula, though. He spits up a lot and is generally pissed off most of the time. Maybe we should try soy?

7/15/2003—Soy seems to be working okay, but he still seems a bit colicky. He's very irritated a lot and has a constant runny nose. Is this normal?

7/28/2003—Today was a great day!! Justin smiled the sweetest little smile at me and it totally motivated me to write a poem about it. He seemed unusually happy today. Guess he's getting used to the soy formula. Or maybe it's just gas???

7/30/2003—Another fun day of shots for Justin. It was the same round as last time, with the exception of no Hepatitis B. Justin ran a slight fever and slept most of the afternoon.

8/1/2003—Justin has been very congested and coughing since he got his shots on 7/30. Why is he so sick all of the time? He woke up this morning covered in a red rash—small raised red bumps. His fever got up to 101, but after I gave him some Tylenol, it seemed to stabilize. The doctor said not to worry unless his fever goes higher or if he has vomiting or diarrhea. She also said we need to put Justin on a nebulizer to help with the congestion. Also, she warned that he may be developing asthma.... great ...

9/10/2003—Well, we've been trying desperately to get Justin through all the congestion and coughing with the nebulizer treatments, but it's so hard to get him to sit through it. It makes him really mad and upset, which makes the congestion and coughing worse because he's screaming!! He sounds like a little old man, with that constant rattle in his chest, so once again we had to take him back to the doctor.

9/15/2003—Justin is still spitting up a lot. Guess it's time to go back to the doctor again..... .

9/19/2003—Finally got in to see the doctor. She said we should try having Justin sleep in the car seat—even in the crib. It will help his digestion and lessen the spitting up all the time. Hey—at least I'm getting some nice biceps thanks to all the lifting of the car seat. That sucker is heavy!

9/22/2003—The car seat thing seems to be working well and we're all getting a little bit more sleep. Ahh, sweet, sweet sleep.

9/29/2003—Justin received his next round of vaccinations today, with the same schedule as last time: DPT, Polio, HIB and Pneumococcal. Once again, slight fever and sleepy/restless the rest of the day.

9/30/2003—Justin has been in a rotten mood today. He just doesn't seem to feel well. It's very depressing.

10/10/2003—There's been lots of congestion and runny nose symptoms for the past few weeks. The nebulizer helps a little, but not nearly enough.

10/18/2003—Other than the sinus issues, Justin has been so happy for the last few days. He giggles at everything and just seems like such a happy baby. Thank God he's feeling better now!!

10/22/2003—So much for the happy baby. He's sick again. He's been vomiting all morning.

10/27/2003—Justin is such a little doll. He's rolling over and he can actually get around like that. If I set him on the edge of the blanket and leave the room, I come back and he's across the room! He's like a little steam-roller.

11/20/2003—Justin and I had a little photo session today, trying to get a good shot for Christmas cards. He's pushing up and trying to crawl, and always seems to have a smile on his face. I put a Santa hat on him with his diaper and red socks. Precious!!

12/29/2003—Poor Justin got his third Hepatitis B shot today. He was pretty upset with me for the rest of the day.

2

What's Happening To My Little Boy?

When Justin was eleven months old, he came down with a severe case of stomach flu. He had just gotten over yet another upper respiratory infection and I think we had gone all of one or two days without the typical drippy nose, congestion and cough that we had become so accustomed to.

This particular morning, Justin woke up with a distinct pallor to his pale complexion that was perfectly ashen and green—all at the same time. He was overly thirsty and immediately drank an entire bottle of water. And then, I got the look.

You know the look I'm talking about? It's that look from your child when their stomach is contracting in pain. The skin gets all flushed, sweaty and pale all at the same time. It's the look that says, "Uh, oh, better give me some room here."

That's when the vomiting started. We gave him Pedialite. He vomited. We gave him water. He vomited. We gave him Gatorade. He vomited. It was like a scene from The Exorcist. My poor little baby couldn't keep anything down all day long and by nighttime, we finally broke down and took him to the emergency room.

The emergency room was a nightmare. The doctors had trouble getting an IV started on him and kept poking him over and over again. It was awful. Once they finally got him on the drip, they rehydrated him and sent us home with a warning to keep an eye on him. If he started vomiting again, we were to bring him right back to the hospital.

Well none of us slept much that night. Justin wanted to be held all night long and whimpered for most of the next twelve hours. He faded in and out of sleep and was so weak and in such obvious discomfort that my heart broke every time I looked at his little face.

The next morning was not much better. He started vomiting up what looked to me like coffee grounds. I immediately panicked because I remembered one of the nurses saying that anything that dark of a color would probably mean he was vomiting blood. We high-tailed it back to the emergency room and they admitted us on the spot.

For the next two days, we stayed at the hospital with Justin, completely frantic and virtually helpless. Doctors were in and out of our room all day and all night, faces grim and impassive. I have never been so scared, yet my heart was so full of love for this child, I thought it would burst. Ultimately, the virus ran its course and finally on day three, Justin was strong enough to go home again. I will never forget the look on his face when he was covered in tubes and so distraught. That look will haunt me for the rest of my life.

This episode was only the beginning of a string of gastrointestinal issues that would begin to worsen over the next two years. I was so busy during that time, trying to keep my full-time job, be a good mother, taking care of a very sick little boy, all while moving into a new house. I had divorced Justin's father and was overwhelmed, dealing with the daily guilt of being a single working mother. I didn't understand that a very frightening pattern in my son's health was developing as well.

The pattern that I can see so clearly now was due to Justin's immune system being overwhelmed almost from birth. *Remember that first Hepatitis B shot?* His immune system was so overwrought from the time he was two weeks old, so busy trying to deal with the toxic overload of mercury and other vaccination additives that it was unable to deal with anything else.

This is especially significant because if you can treat metal toxicity early enough, you can oftentimes stop or even reverse some of the damage that's been done. But you have to know what to look for and what kinds of questions to ask in order to make sure you're treating the right problem.

If your child, like Justin, has been overwhelmed with a mega-dose of mercury, then he's going to need extra help in getting back to having any sort of normal health status. Make no mistake. Any amount of mercury in a developing infant is dangerous. "Mercury," according to Dr. Blaylock of the Blaylock Wellness Report, "is a unique poison in that it incapacitates numerous enzymes in cells, including those used to neutralize free radicals."

"In addition," Dr. Blaylock continues, "mercury blocks the removal of glutamate from the nervous system. By paralyzing this removal system, mercury triggers chronic excitotoxicity—that is, chronic destruction of the nervous system."[2]

So you have to remove the blockage, bolster the immune system and improve the child's nutrition in order for the body to re-learn how to process everything correctly. Simply put, nutrition is the easiest part of the equation. It is the master key to maintaining all of the complex systems inside a baby's body. And when our kid's bodies are already struggling with heavy metal toxic overload, it's time to go back to the basics and start over.

3

My Little Einstein

Justin, though small at birth, was gaining weight and height at the same rate as his peers. His head seemed a bit large, but we assumed that was due to paternal genetics. He met most of his milestones in an acceptable manner, with rolling over, sitting up, smiling, walking and talking—all slightly delayed but close enough to be considered within the normal range of development.

He even said his first clear word on time. Although the vain side of me was hoping and expecting it to be "Mommy", I was almost as happy to hear "Ball" come out of his mouth as clear as day, one afternoon when he was scooting after a ball on the patio. He had been babbling for several months, but this was the first clear connection made and spoken about something we were doing.

His vocabulary increased over the next few months, but then seemed to hit a plateau. He kept speaking only those few words and his range didn't seem to expand at nearly the pace it had started at. Mostly, he just babbled constantly in something resembling a cross between Taiwanese and Swahili.

As the months went by, he learned several words to name things (nouns) and could label just about anything, but that's where his language development stalled. He didn't make the natural transition from one-word sentences, to two-word sentences, to three words, and so on and so forth. Verbs didn't seem to be a part of his unique language.

In between the colds and ear aches, the fevers and diarrhea, Justin was a very happy toddler. I was concerned that he might be falling behind on some of his developmental milestones, but his pediatrician assured me that he was just fine. He kept telling me that boys develop slower than girls and that we should "just wait and see how it goes".

So that's what I did.

I already had my hands full with the difficult divorce and the move and still trying to hold down a very demanding full-time job, so it never dawned on me that I should question the doctor's advice. I kept hoping and assuming that Justin would simply come around on his own and in his own due time.

I started researching child development and playing educational games with Justin. I was overjoyed that he learned to count to ten and then twenty without much effort. Then we started working on the alphabet. Once again, he learned the entire alphabet with ease, but then I noticed he would recite it repeatedly—especially if he was in an uncertain or stressful environment. It's almost like that was a comfort zone for him.

Not to worry, said the doctor once more. *The fact that he learned those things so early on and with such ease shows you just how smart he is.* I wanted to believe what the doctor was saying—so, to put it simply, I did.

It was about this time that the daycare started reporting to me that when Justin was playing, he would often trip on things and rarely put his hands out in front of him to break his fall. He seemed to be a very clumsy kid and almost always had a knot on his forehead from falling on the playground or running into things. I thought that was normal, so once again I chose to ignore the warning signs.

The daycare then started reporting that Justin would "zone out" a lot and usually had several staring spells throughout the day. I had noticed the same thing at home on occasion, but I thought he was just bored or concentrating really hard on something. Now I was not so sure.

The daily afternoon trip to the daycare for pick up soon became a nightmare. I literally started dreading walking into the classroom, because I knew there would be some sort of a report in his backpack from one of the teachers. I still thought that maybe all of this was due to the recent move and divorce, and was trying not to be overly concerned.

After all, if his pediatrician wasn't concerned, why should I be?

I know what you're thinking. It's called denial. And you're right. I kept hoping and praying Justin would outgrow these things and suddenly become a normal child. Unfortunately, that didn't happen.

He became absolutely obsessed with the Baby Einstein videos that I played every day, staring intently at the television and walking back and forth repeatedly while they were on. I thought that was a good thing. To me, the videos were entertaining and educational, so I bought all of them and rotated through each of them every week, thinking it had to be better than watching cartoons.

I noticed he would rarely say anything when he was watching the videos, but seemed to be studying them closely, taking it all in. He never sat still, though. He was in constant motion, walking back and forth, and building endless pillow stacks over and over again.

If I called his name, I rarely got a response. I had to turn off the video to get a response, and that would typically result in a terrible tantrum every time. I couldn't get him to communicate with me without throwing a tantrum. When I asked the doctor about it, the doctor told me, *Welcome to the terrible two's.*

He failed to mention, however, the Terrible Three's and the Terrible Four's....

Although I was aware of these peculiarities with my son, I tried not to dwell on it. I decided that he was just a very unique child and was developing a somewhat quirky personality. Little did I know how quirky he would become or what that would ultimately mean for me and the rest of the family.

4

The Daymare

One of the stranger stories regarding Justin's health is the one where he and I had gone out to Georgetown with my parents (aka Grandma and Papa) to look at their new house that was being built. Justin must have been close to two years old at this time.

It was a very cold fall day. We had just driven up to the front of their new house when I smelled a rather questionable odor. Upon closer inspection, I found out that Justin had had a bit of a "blowout".

This was not your typical blowout, either. This was the foulest, runniest, nastiest kind of blowout you've ever seen. I told Mom & Dad to go on in and look around their house and that I would stay out in the car and change Justin. They happily agreed.

Well, as I took off Justin's pull-up, he had indeed had a blowout and this one was a doozy! It had blown out both sides of the pull-up and all down both legs. So when I took off his pants, there was stuff everywhere, on Justin, on me, on the car seat, on the one and only clean pull-up I had brought with me. It was everywhere.

I opened up the little travel wipes, and there were NONE!!! Yikes!!!

So now I'm stressed out, there's poop everywhere, no wipes and no clean pull-ups or clothes. And it's freezing out there in the car. I start yelling for Mom, but she's at the back side of the house and can't hear me.

So now I'm yelling, Justin starts crying and screaming and squirming, there's still poop everywhere and we're freezing. Fortunately, Mom came out to see what was taking us so long and took over for me. She's such a pro!

She opened the trunk and pulled out a box of wipes, along with an old grocery bag for the smelly stuff. She ushered me out of the car and totally cleaned everything up. I swear—MacGyver has nothing on this lady. Give her a Kleenex and some chewing gum, and she could probably build a Lear jet☺

So we agreed that it's time to go back home and we headed back to their old house. Justin was now in a great mood, since he was probably at least five pounds lighter. I was in a bad mood because I was stressed out and still covered in poop.

Back at home, Mom lent me some fresh clothes and told me to go take a shower. She fed us lunch and then sent me and Justin upstairs to take a nap. But it doesn't end there. It only gets more bizarre.

We went upstairs to the guest room and Justin fell asleep on my chest. I tried to go to sleep too, but after about fifteen minutes, it's just not happening for me. So I started gingerly trying to get out from under Justin without waking him up.

Just as I've almost succeeded in escaping unnoticed, I got a little tickle in my throat and coughed softly. Justin woke up, but not all the way. He startled and then started screaming.

His eyes were open, but he was acting really weird. I mean really weird as in violent. He was pushing at me and telling me "Stop it", but then he would frantically grab at me too like he was scared and didn't want to let go of me.

It sort of freaked me out and I didn't know what to do. He was in this weird manic rage which went on for at least ten minutes. No matter what I did, I couldn't calm him down. I finally picked him up and took him downstairs, kicking and screaming the whole way. He was pulling at me and at himself and I was thinking that maybe his tummy was hurting or he had really bad gas from the diarrhea earlier.

My Dad started calling out his name trying to get him to snap out of it, but nothing was working. He just kept on crying and screaming and pushing and pulling at me. Finally my mother ran into the room and immediately went to the kitchen to get some ice chips.

Once again, Grandma to the rescue.

She forced a few of the ice chips into his mouth and sure enough, he snapped out of it. He blinked a few times, then looked around at everyone and said, "Hi, mommy". It was really strange, like he just woke up from a really deep sleep. Then he started watching cartoons and was perfectly fine after that.

In Summary

During the first two years of my son's life, I was simply a new mother trying desperately to juggle all of the demands of motherhood, coupled with the difficulties of mothering a very sick child. Even though I thought I was educated enough to know what I was doing, I really had no idea. So, like most new mothers, I did the best I could with what I had.

When my baby started developing his chronic illnesses with the resulting language, gastrointestinal and behavior issues, I didn't have any notion that it was a much more serious problem. I didn't see or understand how all of it tied together. Obviously, neither did my son's own doctor. *And if your child's doctor doesn't get it—how are you supposed to?*

Looking back, this whole situation reminds me of a little anecdote that you've probably heard many times before. It's about a man who believed that no matter what happened to him, God would save him.

I don't remember all of the details, but it had to do with a man's house being flooded and how he refused to evacuate, even after a neighbor came by to help him, then a policeman, then finally a rescue helicopter. Each time, the man would refuse the help, saying that "God will save me".

Finally, the flood overtook his home and the man died. As he was standing at the Pearly Gates, he demanded to know why God had let him die. "How could you let me die?" he pleaded. "Why didn't you save me?"

God replied, "What are you talking about? I tried to save you three times. Who do you think sent the neighbor, the policeman, and the helicopter to your house?"

The moral of this whole story is … if you see the signs, please read them. Someone just might be trying to tell you something.

Toddlerhood

"Making the decision to have a child—it's momentous. It is to decide forever to have your heart go walking outside your body."

—Elizabeth Stone

5

The Downward Spiral

Justin's second and third years of life were a whirlwind of changes, doctor's visits, antibiotics and alternating bouts of pure happiness, bewildering illnesses and bad behavior. It was beginning to become clear to me that there was something really wrong with my child, but none of the symptoms were extreme enough to explain definitively what that "something wrong" was.

At thirteen months, Justin received his first measles, mumps, rubella shot (MMR) and from there forward, his health took an even more alarming nosedive. Back then, I didn't understand what was happening. Now I know that his first Hepatitis B vaccination at nineteen days old that was so grossly full of the neuro-toxic preservative Thimerosal completely overwhelmed his immune system and set up a chain reaction in his little body for being sick all of the time.

Then the introduction of the MMR virus in his vaccination at thirteen months magnified the downward spiral of health complications that involved the malfunction of multiple bodily systems and organs within my son. The subsequent sicknesses that were treated with antibiotics then caused an enormous amount of yeast to build up in my son's gastrointestinal tract, which then caused intermittent bouts of vomiting, constipation, diarrhea and multiple allergic reactions to both environmental and food irritants.

In a study called, *Mercury, Lead and Zinc in Baby Teeth of Children with Autism Versus Controls*, the authors state that, "Antibiotic use is known to almost completely inhibit excretion of mercury in rats due to alteration of gut flora. Thus, higher use of oral antibiotics in children with autism may reduce their ability to excrete mercury. Higher usage of oral antibiotics in infancy may also partially explain the high incidence of chronic gastrointestinal problems in individuals with autism."3

21

But, here's the thing. Children don't need oral antibiotics if their immune systems are working properly. *So, the question is—what was the beginning factor that set up this domino effect of disaster within Justin's body?*

And we're back again to his first Hepatitis B vaccination. I'll say it again. I believe the initial mega-dose of mercury in Justin's first vaccination crippled his immune system, which then made him chronically sick. This, coupled with the resulting overuse of antibiotics, slowed down Justin's overall development and finally, three years later, resulted in his diagnosis of autism.

And, just think, all of this could have been avoided if the pharmaceutical companies had been willing to spend just a little bit more money on manufacturing their vaccines in single dose vials.

As you'll see from the following journal entries, this was a very challenging time for us. It's amazing that we made it through this time at all.

3/19/2004—It's been about 3 weeks since Justin's hospital stay and he's bogged down again with cough and congestion. He's been sick like this for almost a week. I took him to see the doctor who treated him at the hospital. He said Justin has bronchitis and gave us a prescription for an antibiotic called Zithromax.

4/12/2004—Justin is really sick again with cough, congestion, gagging, no appetite, runny nose and sleeplessness. I hate seeing him like this and don't understand why he's always so sick! Doctor prescribed Zithromax again, along with a cough syrup called Albuterol which should help with the wheezing too.

4/15/2004—Justin took his first steps by himself today. He's so cute; he looks like a little old man who's had too much to drink!

4/26/2004—Justin got his MMR shot today, but once again there were other shots lumped together with it, including Varicella and PPD.

4/29/2004—Justin has developed a red rash on his arms and legs that started yesterday. He's been running a low fever with congestion for two days and he's starting to scratch at the rash. He's very whiny and fussy, but other than that, has been acting pretty normal. I tried to get in to see the doctor but they couldn't work me in.

4/30/2004—My little guy has been sick for the last three days. He's so congested he can hardly breathe and the rash is much brighter and more apparent today. He's covered in it; it looks like he's got a really bad sunburn. He's so uncomfortable that I took him back to the doctor. They worked him in this time and said to give him Benadryl to see if that would help. By evening, he finally started feeling better.

6/28/2004—Well, he's sick again. He woke up this morning with red, matted watery eyes, and a runny nose. The doctor put him on antibiotics again—this time for congestion and ear infection. His eyes are infected too. They gave him prescriptions for amoxicillin and sulfacetamide.

7/7/2004—His congestion and ear infection have turned into bronchitis again with increased cough and chest congestion. We just can't shake this thing! Now the doctor put him on Omnicef to clear it up.

7/30/2004—Justin's been pulling at his ears a lot and his eyes are red and gummy again. His nose is running constantly with a thick, yellowish discharge. Took him to the doctor and they said it's bronchitis again. This time they put him on something called Augmentin. All of these antibiotics and nothing seems to be working. I don't get it.

8/20/2004—I hated to even take Justin in for his next round of shots, but I can't have him in daycare without them! He got DTaP and HIB today.

8/31/2004—Here we go again with the cough, congestion, runny nose. He's had awful nasal drainage in the mornings with the thick, yellowish stuff again for several days. The doctor said it's a viral upper respiratory infection and put him on Balamine and Tylenol.

9/24/2004—I started Justin at a new daycare today. I'm so excited because they seem to have a really good program and they are very happy to have him. I hope this works out better for him, because he didn't seem to do well at the last one.

9/26/2004—Daycare report—Justin fell and hit his head on the playground. They seem concerned that Justin doesn't typically put his hands out in front of him when he falls.

9/29/2004—Justin's little penis has been red and irritated for two days. I took him to the doctor who said he has a bacterial infection. He put him on Clotrimazole, Mupirocin and Ibuprofen.

10/19/2004—Justin has bronchitis again with the awful congestion and cough, along with a heartbreaking wheezing noise. This time they put him on Amoxycillin, Prednisolone and ProCof cough syrup.

10/30/2004—Here it is—two weeks later and Justin is sick again. This time the doctor said "upper respiratory infection" and put him on Omnicef again. This cannot be normal to be sick this much. I'm beginning to wonder if these doctors know what they're doing.

11/9/2004—Daycare report—Justin fell and hit his head on the playground again. This time he got a pretty big cut on his forehead. I rushed him to the doctor and had to help them push the cut together while they put a liquid bandage (Dermabond?) on it. It was excruciating because he was screaming the whole time.

11/18/2004—Daycare report—fell and hit head on playground again.

12/1/2004—Daycare report—fell and hit head on playground again.

12/17/2004—Daycare report—fell and hit head on playground again.

1/11/2005—Justin has been sick for four days with cough, fever, congestion, the usual. The doctor said another upper respiratory infection and pharyngitis. She prescribed Amoxycillin and Tylenol for the fever.

2/9/2005—Justin had a major incident today with bad diarrhea, and then a weird rage when he woke up early from a nap. I couldn't tell if he was having a seizure or was still asleep and having a nightmare.

2/15/2005—Justin has had a weird itchy rash again yesterday and today—covering his arms and legs. He's had a fever too, but staying under 101. He's very whiny and pretty much inconsolable. He's also got an ear infection. The doctor put him on Rocephin and Motrin. Both of his little ears are really red.

2/16/2005—The rash seems better today. Justin slept most of the day.

2/17/2005—Went back to the doctor. His rash is better, but other symptoms are worse. He put him on Omnicef and more Motrin.

2/22/2005—Daycare report—fell and hit head on playground.

2/26/2005—Back to the doctor again with cough and congestion. Looks like it's another upper respiratory infection and prescription for Zithromax. This is ridiculous!

3/8/2005—Daycare report—fell and hit head on playground.

3/9/2005—We had another "night terror" or "daymare" today when the phone rang and woke Justin up early from his nap. He had only been asleep for about 20 minutes when this happened. It took forever to calm him down again. I don't understand what's happening to my little boy and the doctors seem unconcerned.

3/11/2005—Daycare report—fell and hit head on playground. I called the doctor to discuss why Justin keeps falling and what we should do about it. I mean, come on guys, he's fallen on his forehead three times in the last 2 weeks. This can't be normal!! The doctor was rather evasive (what a shock!). When I kept questioning him, he finally said, "keep observing him and if the problem persists, you can always have him seen by a neurologist". But, once again, he didn't seem particularly concerned and totally made me feel like an over-reactive mother.

4/12/2005—Justin received his Hepatitis A shot today. For once, there wasn't much of a reaction. Maybe because it was just one shot instead of five???

5/2/2005—Daycare report—fell and hit head on playground.

6/17/2005—Justin is sick again with more chest congestion and coughing. It's another upper respiratory infection and they prescribed amoxicillin for him.

7/8/2005—Justin has an ear infection again.

8/1/2005—Justin had diarrhea really bad a few days ago and now he has what seems to be an earache. Guess it's time to see the doctor again. Hey, we almost went a whole month without a doctor's visit. *Almost*. The doctor put him on Omnicef again for the ear infection

9/9/2005—Well, Justin has another ear infection. This time they put him on Amoxycillin and Clavulanate.

9/27/2005—I took Justin in to see the doctor again because I can't take this anymore. I'm paying for a daycare that I can't take him to most of the time because he's too sick. I'm about to be fired from my job any day now because I can't work a full week since Justin's sick all the time. Justin woke up this morning with a horrible diaper rash, and I'm certain now that he has a speech delay and other issues. He's always reciting things over and over again and is constantly doing repetitive tasks.

My Dad thinks he might be autistic, but the doctor says my Dad "must have too much time on his hands. There's nothing autistic about your son." The doctor decided we should evaluate Justin's hearing and possibly think about having him seen by an allergist and possibly a neurologist as well.

10/3/2005—Daycare report—Justin tried to bite other children today on three different occasions. Apparently this has been happening over the last several months intermittently, but this is the first I've heard about it.

10/7/2005—Initial consult with an allergist.

10/12/2005—Daycare report—Justin tried to bite twice today.

10/13/2005—Daycare report—Justin fell and hit his head on the playground.

10/14/2005—I had Justin's hearing evaluated today.

10/19/2005—Follow up with the allergist/ENT specialist. He said the hearing test came back normal but Justin does have a lot of sinus issues. We should consider allergy testing and possibly allergy shots. I can't even imagine subjecting Justin to regular shots and more doctor visits at this point.

6

Early Childhood Intervention

11/5/2005—I finally called ECI (Early Childhood Intervention) today and discussed having Justin evaluated for developmental delays. I have his initial evaluation scheduled for 11/9/2005.

ECI (sometimes called Homespun) is a state-sponsored program that helps families who are dealing with a child that has a learning delay. They help by identifying the problem (whether it's language, physical, social or behavior delay) and by creating an individual education program tailored to the unique needs of the toddler. The program is designed to assist families from the birth of their special child until the child turns three. At that time, the child is no longer eligible for their services and their special educational needs are turned over to the local school district.

My experience with ECI:
It had been suggested to me for two months or so that I ought to check with ECI or Homespun and have Justin evaluated for developmental delays. This suggestion was made by my friend's brother who was a former principal of an elementary school and was very familiar with special needs kids. He had met Justin two or three times and encouraged me to have him evaluated. I resisted because I wanted to believe deep down that Justin didn't really have a problem—even though I knew in my heart of hearts that something was wrong. Thankfully, I finally listened to this man and to my own instincts! And thankfully, this man kept prodding me to do something now. "Early intervention is key," he said. I'm so grateful I finally listened and made that call.

I had no idea what to say when I finally made the call, because I really didn't know for sure if something was wrong or not. So what do you say? When the lady asked me why I was calling, I sounded pretty much like an idiot. I said, I think there might be something wrong with my son and would like to have him evaluated. She said, "Does he have a diagnosis from a doctor?" I said, "No, his doctor thinks he's just developing a little slow but is perfectly normal." To which she replied, "Then why are you calling?"

Boy did I feel stupid. So I hung up.

A few days later, I decided to try again. Fortunately, this time I got someone who sort of prompted me along by asking a lot of pertinent questions on what Justin's delay might be and what I thought about what might be going on.

So what I want you to know is that you need to be better prepared than I was. When you make your call, let them know exactly what your concern is. Is it that your child has stopped talking? Is it that you don't see any progression with your child's abilities? Or maybe your child has a delay somewhere else—with behavioral or social skills. Let them know that you've read about a delay possibly meaning autism, etc. and you need to have your child evaluated.

Also know that getting help now, when your child is less than three years old, could make a profound impact on helping your child overcome any difficulties that might otherwise take a really long time. Don't be bashful and don't be afraid. Don't procrastinate when it comes to your child. I can't stress this enough. Be proactive and get the help you need <u>*now*</u>*!*

11/21/2005—The ECI evaluator went to Justin's daycare and met with Justin's teachers today. They told her that Justin's biting started back in May and has been escalating over the last few months. He has difficulty following directions, is task avoidant, has little eye contact and doesn't put out his hands when he falls. In addition, he often doesn't respond to his name and has little use of language. Tantrums are increasing as well, which at age two and a half are usually starting to decrease rather than increase.

11/28/2005—ECI report—Justin was sitting by himself on the playground—oblivious to other children and non-responsive to the evaluator. His staring spells (zoning out) have been increasing as well.

12/5/2005—Took Justin for his Hepatitis A shot. They decided to hold off because Justin is sick again with thick, yellowish nasal discharge and cough. They prescribed Amoxycillin and said to follow up with the nurse for his shot once he was feeling better.

12/12/2005—At home, Justin is doing better, but at the daycare he's doing much worse. He can't seem to handle the over-stimulation and zones out a lot or throws tantrums. At home he seems to be using more words, and I have taught him to give up the sippy cup and drink from an open cup.

12/14/2005—ECI report—at the daycare Justin is still very task-avoidant, has difficulty following directions, some biting of other kids (or attempts whenever other children come up to him), not napping well and frequent tantrums. He often throws a big tantrum when I'm trying to take him into the building in the mornings. It's heartbreaking, because they are trying really hard to accommodate him and nothing seems to help. His therapist says she thinks he may have sensory integration issues, whatever the heck that is.

12/15/2005—I took Justin to see a pediatric neurologist today, and he immediately ordered an EEG after the exam. We went straight to the hospital and had it done. Justin did so well at the hospital. I was really surprised, because it had been a very long day. The neurologist was running four hours late for our appointment. Four hours!! The doctor had been called to the hospital for an emergency (a boy that was having a grand mal seizure during an operation) but had not bothered to have his staff let all of the people in his waiting room know. So then after our appointment with him, we had to go wait at the hospital. I couldn't believe Justin did as well as he did. When we were in one of the waiting rooms at the hospital, Justin walked around and shook everyone's hands. It was great! I had never seen him do that before. That sure didn't seem like an autistic kid to me..... .

12/19/2005—Took Justin to the doctor for coughing, congestion and general irritability. She started him on Balamine for cough and Zyrtec for allergies.

12/21/2005—ECI report—Justin had heavy tantrums today due to unusually heavy activity (Christmas party). They reported that he had no interaction if a TV was on, some staring spells, little use of vocabulary and spontaneous repetitive activity (called stimming).

12/22/2005—I took Justin in for a CT scan today, which showed no abnormalities other than heavy sinus issues. Once again, he did surprisingly well during the test. What a sweetheart..... .

1/19/2006—Refilled Zyrtec prescription today. It seems to be helping to clear the fog a little bit for Justin. His vocabulary is increasing, but there are still a lot of tantrums and repetitive activity at school.

1/26/2006—ECI report—best session by far. He still had two tantrums today, but his compliance, vocabulary and inclusion with other children seems a little better.

2/3/2006—ECI report—the biting has begun again and is much worse now. He knows it's wrong and will even put himself in a time-out. It seems like he's doing it so he can go in a time-out and not have to be around others kids. I'm telling you, this kid is a genius!!

2/16/2006—ECI report—he's still biting other children, but at least the frequency seems to be decreasing. He's using more vocabulary but still very delayed for his age.

2/20/2006—I took Justin today to be evaluated by the public school's special education department to see if he will qualify for early childhood services once he turns three. It was very hectic, and they suggested that Justin may have high-functioning autism. It was not a diagnosis, exactly, but more a suggestion that he "has certain autistic tendencies". They said he does qualify for services and suggested a six-hour autism class, five days a week. I decided to start out slowly with only a speech therapy class to see how it goes. I do not believe Justin is autistic, but I know he does have some developmental delays. They will evaluate him again at the end of the summer.

2/23/2006—ECI report—Justin is using more words, counting to twenty, reciting the entire alphabet and following directions much better at home.

3/3/2006—Daycare report—Justin fell and hit his head on the playground.

3/4/2006—Justin woke up this morning with fever and vomiting.

3/7/2006—ECI report—The last two days have been a little rough. Justin has bitten three children and has been very cranky.

3/15/2006—ECI report—Justin has been over-stimulated, task-avoidant and has difficulty focusing during circle time at the daycare. He needs constant attention and redirection.

3/23/2006—Justin has been very congested for the last few days, but instead of taking him to the doctor and putting him on more antibiotics, I'm treating him with over the counter medications. So far, it seems to be just as effective.

Justin's Third Birthday

3/31/2006—Wow—we had Justin's birthday party today for his 3rd birthday. What a fiasco. Justin bit three kids, pushed two and had major meltdowns about every three minutes. It was exhausting for me, and he was way over-stimulated the entire time. I'm about at my wit's end.

4/10/2006—**Justin was kicked out of the daycare today for biting three more kids.** They have tried really hard to find a solution for him, but they can no longer take the liability. I understand their position, but now what do I do? I mean, I have to have a daycare for Justin so I can manage to keep my job, so I can have the income (and the insurance) to take care of Justin. I'm doing all of this by myself with little help or child support from Justin's father. I have to take off of work all the time to take Justin to doctor's appointments or stay home with him because he's too sick to be in the daycare. I'm so lucky to have such a wonderful and supportive boyfriend. I don't know what I would do without Dave. What do all of the other single parents do? I know I'm not the only one dealing with this kind of situation …

4/11/2006—Justin woke up with fever, diarrhea and vomiting again this morning. He had a little diarrhea last night, and I'm guessing that's why he was biting kids yesterday. Maybe his little stomach was cramping??

4/14/2006—Mom kept Justin for a few days so I could have a much-needed break and try to find a new daycare. This afternoon, we decided to meet halfway at a restaurant so I could pick Justin up, and we could have a nice dinner together—with Dave and his two girls and my parents and aunts and uncles.

When we arrived at the restaurant, I could hardly wait to see Justin—I missed him so bad. I ran up to Mom (who was holding Justin on her lap) and reached out to hug Justin tight. He looked right past me like he didn't even recognize me. I was heartbroken. After about ten minutes, Justin finally looked at my face and it dawned on him that it was me. He smiled a huge smile and said "Mommy!" and hugged me really tight. It was very peculiar, because I had been there for at least ten minutes before he recognized me. Then halfway through our meal, he had a major meltdown and we had to leave the restaurant.

After I finally got Justin to bed, I found an article on Penn State's website that quoted the Director of the National Institute of Health and Human Development at a speech given at the National Autism Conference in 2002. It said, "(Research shows …) Young children with autism often fail to show normal facial recognition. Very young children don't recognize their mother's face, but do show normal recognition of familiar objects. The neural systems that mediate face recognition exist very early in a child's life, offering the possibility that facial impairment may be one of the earliest indicators of abnormal brain development in autism."[4]

I would like to say that the article made me feel much better, but I am still devastated.

4/17/2006—I found a new daycare with a lady that keeps six kids in her home. Today was Justin's first day, and he seemed to do really well.

4/20/2006—Justin started speech therapy today with the school district. The class will be for thirty minutes once a week. His teacher seems very patient and kind, so maybe she'll be able to get through to him and make a difference.

4/28/2006—Justin received two shots today—pneumococcal and Hepatitis A. No major incidents.

5/1/2006—Daycare report—bit a child.

5/4/2006—Daycare report—bit a child.

5/5/2006—Daycare report—tried to bite 2 kids.

5/18/2006—Justin has bitten at the daycare at least 3–4 times this week.

5/19/2006—Justin was kicked out of daycare for the second time for biting. I'll be taking yet another week off of work so I can try to find a new daycare again.

5/29/2006—Dave and I have decided to get married and tackle the challenge of raising Justin together. I finally feel like I have the support I need to get through this. Justin and I are very, very lucky, and I feel so blessed to have Dave in my life.

6/5/2006—Justin started at a new home-based daycare today part-time. I've had to reduce my work schedule to three days per week. I've been able to talk the school into extending Justin's speech therapy for six more sessions during the summer since he's just starting to make some progress there.

6/8/2006—Justin woke up with fever and vomiting/diarrhea. I stayed home with him again today.

6/20/2006—I hired a part-time nanny to be home with Justin when I'm at work, since he's not doing so well around other kids.

6/22/2006—Justin woke up with diarrhea, vomiting and fever. It was the same as the last few times. He wakes up very thirsty and drinks an entire cup of water or juice. Then the vomiting starts and lasts for four or five hours. Then he seems fine and eats normally the rest of the day. I had to stay home with him again today.

7/13/2006—We're back to the cough, congestion and nasal discharge. I stayed home again today.

7/16/2006—I finally started potty training Justin. He's doing really well and I'm hoping to have him fully trained by the end of the summer.

8/1/2006—I bought a copy of Love & Logic today and have started implementing some of the concepts. (Read the next chapter for more details.) The principles seem to work well with Justin, so I'm beginning to have some hope in managing his challenging behavior.

8/21/2006—Justin started a PDD class at the local elementary school. PDD stands for Pervasive Developmental Disorder and basically means the child has a developmental delay of some kind, whether it's speech, social skills or general behavior. For Justin, it's all three. The class is for two hours/day and five days/week and incorporates some speech therapy and some occupational therapy. I'm hoping this will work for him so he doesn't have to go to the autism class. I have observed the autism class twice, and though the teachers are amazing with the kids, it seems like most of the kids are much more severely disabled than Justin. I'm worried that he might pick up some of the bad behavior, and it will do more harm than good. I'm not sure what I should do.

8/23/2006—School report—Justin threw a major temper tantrum and threw his head back and hit the floor. He injured his head, and it had to be iced down in the nurse's office.

9/1/2006—After a rare long weekend at his Dad's house (two nights), Justin came home and was no longer potty-trained and was also suddenly afraid of the dark. He was afraid to go to sleep and was very clingy and whiny for the next several days like he was scared of something.

10/18/2006—Justin's progress report from his school was evasive at best. It mentioned "some improvement" but mostly that Justin is having a really hard time with transitions. They do a lot of activities within the two hour class each day, and he cannot seem to transition from one activity to the next. He tantrums nearly every day, and the teacher is not sure what to do with him. It's being highly-suggested again that I consider putting him in the longer, more-comprehensive autism class. They have a 2:1 ratio of children to teachers, and they think he would do much better in that environment.

10/20/2006—Justin woke up this morning with major vomiting until noon. Then he was starving and ate like a little piggy for the rest of the day.

10/26/2006—Justin woke up this morning with a lot of congestion and coughing. It seemed like a cold so I decided to treat with over-the-counter medications. I just don't want him on any more antibiotics unless absolutely necessary.

11/03/2006—I attended a meeting at Justin's school today to discuss teacher and parent concerns over his erratic behaviors, impulsivity, limited attention to instruction, poor eye contact and impaired social interaction. Outcome of the meeting was a diagnosis of autism and speech impairment, along with the suggestion for Justin to attend the autism class in the spring semester (after holiday break).

11/5/2006—I've begun giving Justin clay detox baths to see if he might have some environmental pollutants in his system that the clay can pull out of him. I really believe there's something going on inside his body that can be treated—other than a general "possibly autistic" diagnosis. After his very first detox bath, he seemed much more alert and connected. I was showing him Baby Einstein flash cards, and he started joking around with me and answering my questions with really funny answers.

I showed him a picture of a cow and said, "Justin, this is a cow. Cows eat grass. This cow is black and white." Then I asked him, "Justin what kind of animal is this?" He looked at the picture, then looked at me and said, "A cat." And he totally cracked up. Then I said, "Justin this is a cow. What do cows eat?" And again, he looked at the picture, then looked at me, and said, "Cookies". And he cracked up again. Priceless.

This was the first clear sign to me that there might be some real hope for my son's future.

7

Love and Logic

Outside of the horrific health problems that parents often have to deal with in autistic kids, there is the even more frustrating issue of their erratic, exhausting and, let's face it, irritating behavior.

Oprah did a show on autism several months ago, and I remember hearing one mother say that her son was literally driving her crazy with his nutty behavior. And it's true. Their behavior is so oftentimes bizarre and filled with such high-energy hyperactivity that it can be an absolute drain on even the most doting and loving parents. It can literally feel like you're being sucked into a huge pit of quicksand, pretty much on a daily basis.

I know, because there have been many times in the past when I literally wanted to scream at Justin to stop whatever odd behavior he was doing, because I really didn't think I could take it anymore. I can't tell you how many times I've felt like locking myself in the hall closet or walking out the front door and never coming back. Sounds crazy, doesn't it?

Only those who have really been there can really understand what I'm saying. But we somehow manage to keep it together day in and day out, because most of us realize we're the only ones our kids really have. We are pretty much their only ticket to the outside world, so we have to constantly pull ourselves together and trudge forward through the daily frustration, anger and guilt in order to help them find their way too.

So, you may be wondering, what finally helped me with Justin's behavior?

One of the best things I've found is a book called, Love and Logic: Magic for Early Childhood, which focuses on parenting with humor and from a loving point of view. This book made sense to me, plain and simple, and I would highly recommend it. I don't receive any sort of proceeds and I have no relationship with the authors of the book, but I simply like to share with other parents what has worked well for me.

Children, in general, and autistic kids in particular, have issues with lack of control. But then again, you may be thinking, don't we all? And you're right. Most of us need to feel some sense of control or else we start feeling like we're losing our grip on reality.

Imagine how that must feel for an autistic child.

A lot of toddlers go through the terrible twos or the terrible threes because they don't yet have the verbal acuity to express themselves. They whine or cry because they don't know how else to display their displeasure. It's the same for autistic kids, only they may be five, six, seven or beyond and still throwing tantrums to get what they want.

It may seem as if these kids are being bratty or undisciplined, but the reality is autistic kids in particular have practically zero control over their environment. That's usually by design, and very necessary for their own protection, but just try to imagine how frustrating it must be for them. In order to gain just a tiny little sense of control, these kids usually throw a tantrum as their way of communicating some of that frustration.

And what happens when a child, whether autistic or not, throws a fit in public?

Typically, the parents are so embarrassed that they give the child whatever it is they want so the kid will pipe down. The problem with that is it reinforces in the child's mind exactly what it takes to get what they want. In essence, it shows the child that throwing a hissy-fit works really well.

Go figure. The child gets the payoff he's looking for, so he does it again, and again, and again.

Now, don't get me wrong. I'm not preaching here. Believe me, there have been plenty of times when I've given in just like you. It's very hard not to, especially when you're somewhere and it's really crowded or you're in a hurry. Justin has certainly had his share of successes and payoffs, that's for sure. However, nowadays they happen less and less frequently.

What the folks from Love and Logic explain very clearly in their book, they explain in relation to normally-developing children. But I believe it has worked wonders with Justin, and it just may do the same for you and your child. It's a simple theory and pretty simple to enforce too.

They believe in giving a child choices. When it's not an important decision, go ahead and let the child choose. A good example is giving your child the choice between two types of vegetables for dinner. You're not letting them choose *if* they will have a vegetable, but rather *which one* of the two will they have?

Why *not* give them a little bit of the control so they can get used to making their own decisions? Let me explain how it works and what I've used with my son. As you'll see, it's great because it helps expand their vocabulary at the same time.

I start out each morning while we're driving to school. I'll say, "Justin, should I drive fast or slow?" Justin doesn't know how fast I'm really going, so if he says fast, I just rev the gas a little bit, and he breaks into giggles. If he says slow, I start talking really slow, saying "Okay, Justin wants to drive slow, so we are driving slow...."

Another one I use is, "Is it rainy or sunny outside?" He's been learning about weather at school, so he really likes this one. I also say things like, "Are you going to have a good day today or a bad day?" He always picks "good".

If you repeatedly ask lots of questions to your child and get lots of answers or "choices", then when it's time for a big decision, like going to bed, you won't get as much resistance when it's your turn to make the choice. It doesn't mean your child is suddenly going to start skipping off to bed if this has been a point of contention for quite some time, but it should start making the process a little bit easier on you.

I mean, does it really matter to you if Little Johnny takes a bath *before* dinner or *after* dinner? I'm guessing, probably not. But by you allowing your child to feel just a little bit more in control of their environment, it should work to empower them and in return make them just a little bit more agreeable with everything else.

Here are some more examples of choices I now give Justin on a daily basis:

- "Do you want to go to the bathroom now or in five minutes?" He almost always says "five minutes".

- "Do you want to take your bath now or go to bed now?" He will always say "bath", because he doesn't want to go to bed yet. Before I tried this concept, it would be at least a thirty or forty minute process just to get him into the tub.

- "Do you want an apple or a banana for your fruit?" Instead of saying "do you want a piece of fruit?", which would usually be met with "no", I give him a choice of two fruits and he will always pick one.

- "Do you want to go in the front door or the garage door?" It doesn't make one bit of difference to me, but it gives Justin that all important sense of being in charge.

- You can also use, "Do you want Mommy to put you to bed or Daddy?" This is great, because instead of saying, "Are you ready for bed?", **you** are making the important part of the decision, which is—it's time for bed. Your child gets to decide **who** puts him to bed.

I've been able to cut Justin's bedtime ritual down from about an hour and a half ordeal most nights to about fifteen minutes. If he starts to fuss when I tell him it's time for bed, I just stand up and start walking toward his room and he will always follow. Before trying out this routine, he would throw himself on the ground and cry and fuss for 20–30 minutes, thereby delaying going to bed and in essence getting what he wanted. Now we take that possibility out of the equation.

Another thing that's worked really well with Justin is to hold off giving him what he wants until he phrases his request properly. This has worked wonders for his language development. Case in point is his fondness for the game of chase. He loves to be chased around the room to the point of exhaustion. I mean this kid could go for hours.

I used to always say, "Mommy's gonna getcha!" whenever I would chase him. (I am a Texan, after all....) So, he started saying, "Mommy getcha!" whenever he wanted to be chased. I would usually respond, and he would take off giggling.

Then one day, I started saying, "Do you want me to chase you?" He would say "yes, Mommy getcha!", but I didn't move. He demanded again, "Mommy getcha!" and I said, "Do you mean Mommy chase me?" He said "Yes, Mommy getcha!", but I didn't move again. I simply repeated "Mommy chase me!" until he repeated it too.

Then I finally got up and chased him around the room. Whenever he made his request the next time, I wouldn't stand up until he said it the right way. Now he always says, "Mommy chase me!"

In Summary

Our kids are so incredibly smart. It's pretty easy for us parents to forget that fact sometimes, especially when we're so used to doing so much for them.

We translate for them. We make excuses for them. We try to compensate for their weaknesses. We try to figure out what they need before they need it. We try to make up for what they're missing. We try to make their crazy, erratic world just a little bit more normal.

With so much busyness going on, it's easy to forget that our kids are highly-evolved, intelligent creatures, probably more so than we will ever realize. That's why it's so important to remember that if we continue to keep our expectations high, I believe they will continue to strive to reach them.

So aim high, Mommies and Daddies, and give your special kids the room they need to surprise you! ☺

Finding Some Answers

"The best and most beautiful things in the world cannot be seen or even touched—they must be felt with the heart.".

—Helen Keller

8

Generation Rescue

On January 7, 2007, my husband called and was very excited about something. In fact, he could barely slow down long enough to explain it to me. That might not seem strange to you, but you have to understand something about my husband, Dave.

The guy is a very calm, quiet, centered man. It's like his middle name is "The Rock" or something. He doesn't typically get overly-excited about things, so I knew this had to be something big.

He had flown to Dallas that day and while he was waiting for the hotel van to pick him up from the airport, our good friend Fate decided to intervene. Don't forget, I'm a big believer in Fate and Destiny and A Bigger Purpose. I'm a sucker for *all* that stuff.

While Dave was waiting for the hotel van, he sat down next to a guy and then realized they knew each other. They had gone through pilot-training together about eight years prior and not seen each other since. They started talking about wives and families, and Dave told him about Justin and all of the challenges we'd been going through for the last year.

We had recently received the general diagnosis from the local elementary school that Justin was "displaying autistic tendencies" and had just made the agonizing decision to place him in the autism class starting in January. The holidays had just ended and I was exhausted.

As Dave was telling his friend about our recent news, his friend pulled out a sheaf of papers the size of a phonebook. He then started telling Dave about *his* daughter, who had also been diagnosed with autism and how they had been treating her successfully with alternative treatments over the last year. He had statistics and medical reports and charts and graphs galore. He excitedly told Dave what we needed to do immediately.

"It's not too late," he said. "You can still help Justin now before he turns five. You have plenty of time to stop and even reverse a lot of the damage that's been done. Tell your wife to go to www.generationrescue.org. Read through the whole website and get yourself a DAN! Doctor right away. Don't waste any more time. You can still save your son."

Immediately after my husband relayed this incredible news, I went straight to the computer and began studying every bit of the Generation Rescue website. It was full of information on autism and the amazing similarities between autism symptoms and the symptoms of heavy metal toxicity. I found out that a DAN! Doctor is a doctor who follows a general protocol established by Defeat Autism Now! That protocol involves treating the child nutritionally with supplements, a restricted diet, various therapies and biomedical testing.

As I read through the testimonials listed on the website, I couldn't believe how many of the kids sounded exactly like Justin. Some of the kids were certainly more severe than my little guy, but there were an awful lot of similarities. I could feel the adrenaline pulsing through me as I frantically scribbled down notes and clicked on the different links listed for additional resources and information.

This was the true ray of hope I'd been looking for—one that I so desperately needed. And here it was—just a chance encounter that could've easily been missed. See why I love Fate so much?

The basic gist of the website was that autism and many other neuro-developmental disorders are caused by a major catalyst that begins a series of problems in a child's body, resulting in multiple symptoms that eventually classify your child as being on the autism spectrum. In many cases, it appears that vaccinations are that catalyst.

For the next three days, I ate, drank and breathed the Internet, searching and researching every connection I could find between vaccinations and autism. There's a lot of information out there, and as I mentioned before, a lot of it is vague and conflicting. You, as a parent, don't know what to believe.

You have to read and study and research, and then come up with your own conclusions in regards to your specific child. I immediately decided that I needed to start supplementing Justin nutritionally. I followed some of the advice given on the Generation Rescue website and some that I had gleaned from other similar websites.

Nutritional Supplements

I knew Justin did not have a fully-rounded, nutritionally-sound diet, so the first thing I did was to order a liquid **vitamin and mineral complex**, specifically designed for kids "on the spectrum". Then I ordered another supplement called L-glutathione, which is something often found deficient in autistic kids.

L-Glutathione

L-glutathione is a natural detoxifier produced by our bodies to help get rid of unwanted toxins that we encounter from our water, food, environment or, say, vaccinations. It provides the body's main cellular defense against oxidative stress. I learned that most autistic kids do not produce enough of it.

The L-glutathione supplement arrived first and I immediately started giving it to Justin sparingly. *Within two days*, I noticed he was much more alert and responsive whenever I asked him a question. I was enthused but still reserved.

The next day I started him on the liquid minerals once a day. The leaflet suggested starting out slow with the minerals first, and then slowly adding in the vitamins. Once I was sure there would be no side effects, I could continue to increase the amount to the full dose based on his body weight.

Omega-3 Fish Oil

The next day I added in a dose of Omega-3 Fish Oil, which I mixed into applesauce. Omega-3 is part of a family of essential fatty acids, responsible for fighting inflammation in the body, facilitating absorption of key nutrients, and detoxifying unwanted compounds more efficiently.

It was January 13th, exactly five days after learning about the Generation Rescue website, and Justin woke up extremely happy and talkative for the first time in a very long time. Ordinarily, I would have to wake him, and he would almost always be in a grumpy mood. I was bolstered in a huge way and very excited, to say the least.

The next day I increased his minerals to 3 times a day and added a small dose of the vitamins, continuing with the fish oil and L-glutathione supplements. That afternoon I noticed for the first time that Justin was mimicking actions on Blue's Clues. He was very chatty and excited, talking out loud at the television and turning and laughing with me. Usually, he would just watch the video without saying anything.

I noticed he was also much more responsive to directions from me. Instead of having to ask him four or five times to do something, he was actually responding on the first request! *This was big, I decided.*

We had a bit of a regression the next day, because the weather had turned very wet, cold and icy overnight and Justin woke up with a runny nose and cough. He was still very happy and chatty, so I went ahead with the vitamin regimen, increasing the dose of liquid vitamins. I was still giving the liquid minerals 3 times a day, the fish oil once a day, and the L-glutathione once a day.

The next night he was not feeling very well due to the runny nose and cough, but surprisingly he was still very talkative and happy. Ordinarily, if he woke up with a cold, he would be whiny, clingy and lethargic. This, I was beginning to realize, was a different child than the child of only a week ago. For the first time ever, *he asked me* if he could go to bed! No more power struggles at bedtime.

By the next day, I noticed his speech was much clearer. He had better enunciation and less jargon. His speech was also becoming much more spontaneous as opposed to him repeating whatever I said (called echolalia) or only answering if I gave him choices. I did notice him being easily frustrated and whiny, but the bonus was he went to the potty consistently at school and at home.

That weekend, I decided we would drive to Georgetown to see my parents. They noticed a tremendous improvement in him—within the first few minutes of us being there. They were amazed at the big difference in vocabulary and in Justin's overall interaction. He ate and slept well, and we all had a really good time. It was January 20th, exactly 13 days after first learning about the Generation Rescue website.

Collecting Medical Records

During this time, I started really delving into Justin's medical history. I pulled together every receipt I could find for doctor's visits, specialists, prescriptions, everything. I organized all of it into a timeline so that I could study it for any patterns. I was amazed at just how sick my little boy had been—especially between one and three years old.

The next step was to make a list of vaccinations he had received over the years, and to find out if any of them contained Thimerosal (the mercury-laced preservative that was known to be neurotoxic to infants). This was easier said than done. Fortunately, doctors are required to write down the date, manufacturer name and lot number of every vaccination given to a child. That was the easy part.

Trying to find out what each of the vaccinations contained in them, however, was not so easy. Most of Justin's shots had been given to him at least two or three years previously and since then, many of the pharmaceutical companies had merged or changed names. In addition, they would not release information to me over the phone. Their reason for withholding this information is—I'm not a physician, only a parent.

Shouldn't a parent have a right to receive this information? After all, we're talking about being able to know what was injected into my own child!!! I persevered anyway and after a full week of wrestling with medical employees in several offices, I finally had a fairly composite list with one glaring fact staring me in the face.

According to the mercury calculator on the National Vaccine Information Center website (www.NVIC.org), the very first vaccination that Justin received when he was only nineteen days old had forty-three times the level of mercury in it that the EPA considers safe. Forty-three times!!! It is horrific for any child to receive something so toxic, but imagine what it did to the internal workings of my tiny little six pound, nineteen-day-old infant.

Once again, Hepatitis B is given primarily for protection against a disease contracted through sexual contact and intravenous drug users. *Why is it being required in newborns? And how could anyone believe that a newborn's immature immune system could possibly handle an injection laced with so much of a known neurotoxin?*

From what I could tell, most of his other vaccinations only contained what they called a "trace amount" of Thimerosal. That was reassuring at first. The problem is that they rarely receive just one shot per visit, and when a baby is receiving multiple shots at one time—each with only a "trace amount" of mercury in it—it adds up to being a lot more than a "trace amount" being injected into their little bodies.

And the results can be absolutely devastating.

According to the information listed on the website for the Agency for Toxic Substances & Disease Registry (ATSDR), children poisoned by mercury may develop problems in their nervous and digestive systems, along with kidney damage. Exposure to high levels of mercury can **permanently** damage the brain and kidneys, resulting in irritability, shyness, tremors, changes in vision or hearing, and memory problems.

And we're injecting this into our kids! What's wrong with this picture?

As I began to talk to friends and family about my findings, I kept getting the same thing over and over again. "How can you be so calm and collected? I would be furious! Have you hired a lawyer yet? This is the most awful, most horrifying thing I've ever heard!!"

But the truth of the matter was, I was ecstatic to know there was something I could do to help my baby. I was overjoyed to know that I could actually help my son recover some of the abilities he had lost. And I was abundantly happy to realize that I would be able to help other parents do the same thing.

I continued treating Justin with supplements and continued to notice his improved speech and behavior. Without question, the consistent frequency of his illness began to diminish. He just seemed to feel better, period. *And* his personality started to blossom. I was beginning to see flashes of character, individuality and intelligence that had previously been hidden for months under the daily behavior and health problems.

It was about this time that I actually began to dream of the possibility of Justin being well enough to go to a regular kindergarten when he turns five.

9

Discovering Justin

As Justin's personality was starting to come out, mine was starting to return to normal as well. I hadn't realized what a toll the stress of caring for a sick child with special needs had taken on me. I started feeling a renewed strength and hope for the future that I hadn't felt in a long, long time.

In my continued quest to assist Justin's recovery, I decided to add an Epsom salt bath to his bedtime routine. I had read about this therapy on the Internet as a way to help relax your child and also to help provide an often-lacking source of magnesium sulfate. Magnesium and sulfates can be ingested from foods or mineral supplements, but both are readily and easily absorbed through the skin in an Epsom Salt bath.

Apparently, a lot of autistic kids have low levels of magnesium and this is one way to help replenish those levels. In addition, many doctors believe that autism is accompanied by bowel disorders that make it difficult to absorb nutrients and to rid the body of wastes. Sulfates have been shown to assist in this process of improving nutrient absorption and toxin elimination.

That evening after Justin went to bed, I went online (like usual) to continue my research. I found a new article that mentioned that although Thimerosal had been removed from most childhood vaccines, it is still commonly found in most flu shots. I think every bit of blood I had drained from my face at that very moment.

Justin had received a flu shot on January 3rd. It was now January 22nd.

I called his pediatrician's office first thing the next morning. Sure enough, the flu shot Justin had received a few weeks before contained 25 mcg of Thimerosal. I was so nauseous—I almost threw up on the spot. I had not even wanted Justin to get a flu shot, but had allowed the doctor to talk me into it. In fact, the doctor had insisted.

I felt so guilty and ashamed of myself for having given in to that doctor. My husband reminded me that I needed to cut myself some slack (something that's rather hard for me to do) and to be glad I learned about all of this prior to his next round of vaccinations. Needless to say, Justin did not get his next round of shots.

Thoughtful House for Children

Thankfully, this is about the time I discovered the Thoughtful House for Children in Austin. It's a biomedical clinic at the forefront of research into children and autism, and how to treat them both nutritionally and medically. They have a comprehensive staff of doctors including a biomedical specialist, gastro-intestinal specialist and nutritionist—all right there, in-house, on staff.

What I found at Thoughtful House is an honest approach in treating these unique and special children. They explain on their website that there is no one cure and that it can be a rather long, expensive process in getting to the root cause of your child's autistic behavior. They know and understand that each child is different and may require a different approach.

Some children have gastro-intestinal distress. Some don't. Some children have major language regression. Some don't. Some children have highly aggressive behavior. Some don't.

That's the frustrating and confounding thing about autism. There's no one-size-fits-all diagnostic tool and no one-size-fits-all therapy. It's truly different for every child and requires a different approach for each child. The staff at Thoughtful House understands that better than anyone else.

On January 29th—just three short weeks after first learning about the website www.generationrescue.org., I had my phone consultation with the new patient in-take specialist at Thoughtful House. We ran through Justin's entire medical, behavioral and physical issues, along with a pretty thorough discussion of his diet.

I was very impressed at how efficient she was on the phone. What a pleasant surprise to be able to get all of the background out of the way before you ever have to step foot in the doctor's office. I wish more doctors would do that.

Our first appointment with Dr. Bryan Jepson was made for Friday, February 9th. It was the same day as my sister's birthday, so I knew that was a good sign. The first thing I noticed when I walked in the front door was the quote over the receptionist's desk.

"Be the change you want to see in the world." Mohandas Gandhi

Wow! I immediately felt a rush of emotion, knowing that we had found the right place to begin Justin's healing. I closed my eyes and said a little prayer of thanks. I was only barely beginning to understand that the biggest hurdle to recovery is the mountain of uncertainty you encounter at every turn. Once you find the right path, however, your strength becomes insurmountable.

I knew I had found the right path.

My mother met me at the doctor's office, so that she could keep Justin entertained while I talked to the doctor. It was almost not even necessary, since Justin focused in on Curious George (the movie) immediately and allowed me to visit with the doctor for almost two hours. I was happy to have her support anyway.

Biomedical Tests

We left with instructions to obtain a stool and urine sample over the weekend and to send it in the special kit they provided for me to take home. Dr. Jepson's concern was that Justin might have some gastrointestinal issues (like most of these kids) and the two tests would give us a pretty clear picture of the next steps we would need to take.

I was to stop the L-glutathione supplement for now, so we could treat any GI issues that showed up on the test results. I was bummed because that was the very first supplement I started giving him *and* it had shown immediate results. The problem with the oral form of L-glutathione, Dr. Jepson explained, is that it can exacerbate a yeast problem in the stomach. So it's best to hold off until the yeast is treated first.

The doctor added calcium, magnesium, zinc and melatonin to Justin's diet and recommended that we make an appointment with their on-staff nutritionist with the understanding that Justin would probably need to go on a gluten-free, casein-free (GFCF) diet very soon. Our appointment with Kelly Barnhill was scheduled for the following week.

That weekend, I had my first experience with trying to collect a sample from my son. I was staying with my parents for the weekend, so at least I had a little moral support. Not that either of them offered to collect the sample for me, you understand, but they were there to help cheer me on nevertheless.

Let me tell you something, if you've never had the pleasure of trying to collect a stool sample (before it hits the water in the toilet) from a child who is barely potty-trained and is not happy about being on the potty in the first place, you're in for quite a treat. I can laugh about it now, but at the time it was just a tad bit stressful!!

The lab reports came in the next week while we were meeting with the nutritionist at Thoughtful House. They indicated that Justin had an imbalance (dysbiosis) of bad gut bacteria to good gut bacteria. In addition, his yeast reading was off the charts. Kelly said that was pretty standard in autistic kids. She also informed us that Dr. Jepson wanted Justin to go GFCF immediately.

We had already started researching the strict diet protocol so were already aware of the difficulty and expense of finding acceptable food alternatives for our finicky son. Kelly gave us lots of insights and advice, though, so we left with a resolve to follow the diet closely.

On March 6th, we had our follow up with Dr. Jepson. He went through the lab test reports with me in detail, confirming what Kelly had already told us and explaining that we needed to do some further testing. He ordered a heavy metals challenge test, so we could have a better idea of what we were really dealing with.

The challenge test would entail a six-hour urine collection on one day, a dose of DMSA (chelation agent) the next day, and then a follow up, post-DMSA six-hour urine collection. The theory is that if heavy metals are present in the body, the first urine will show a baseline, and then the subsequent urine will show more since the DMSA binds to the heavy metals buried deep in the tissues. Once the metals are pulled out of the organs and tissues, the body can then excrete them.

In addition, we decided to do another urine collection to send to a lab in France that would test for porphyrins in his urine. Porphyrins are proteins in our bodies that are responsible for producing certain elements in our blood, called heme. Heme is the carrier protein for iron in hemoglobin, which is what carries oxygen throughout our bodies. Porphyrins also assist the body with the all-important detoxification process.

Without proper production of porphyrins, our bodies are severely compromised in their abilities to detoxify harmful toxins. Mercury and other heavy metals are well-known to significantly impact porphyrin biochemistry. So if Justin's lab tests came back with elevated porphyrin levels, it would be a clear indicator that heavy metal toxicity was involved.

Biomedical Treatments

On Friday, March 9th, we started Justin on Metronidazole—an antibiotic to wipe out the bad bacteria in his gut. It was a seven day treatment. Unfortunately, it would wipe out the good bacteria too, so we needed to add another supplement to his already-burgeoning supplement list. This one was called Mindlinx. It's a probiotic that helps regulate the good bacteria throughout the body.

The following week was Spring Break, which meant the school would be closed, so I took Justin to my parents' house so they could keep him and allow me to work for a few days. I left him off of all supplements, because I knew as soon as I picked him up in three days I would need to have his blood drawn for oxidative stress and a general baseline blood work-up.

This is about where the real challenges set in:

03/13/2007—Mom brought Justin back today and I think she was really ready to drop him off and leave! He's been off of his supplements for the last three days because we have to have his blood drawn to check mineral levels and such, and boy was there a marked difference!! He usually enjoys going to see Grandma and Papa, but this time he was whiny and throwing tantrums at every little thing. He would not listen to them and was generally a very different, difficult little boy from the last time they saw him. I guess that's my validation that he needs those supplements.

03/14/2007—We took Justin to have his blood drawn today. They couldn't find a good vein, so they had to try several times. It was awful. Justin was screaming and we had to hold him down the whole time while they drew four vials of blood. If he hadn't been kicking me so hard, I probably would've passed out. I don't do so well with the sight of blood..... .

03/16/2007—Today is the last day of Spring Break and I am so ready for a vacation of my own. There has been such a major behavior regression this week. Justin was finally happy and chatty again today, but I noticed lots of jargon (gibberish) and he was also very tactile sensitive—meaning lots of roughhousing, chasing, pulling on my shirt, climbing all over me, and bear hugs—or crushes, really. It's exhausting when he gets like this. There was a lot of continuous repeating of words or phrases and then a <u>major</u> meltdown at bedtime. It's almost like he felt that if he just kept repeating that word or phase over and over again, it would finally make sense to me.

I had promised Justin all week long that on Friday we would go to the children's museum and then to the park. From the moment he woke up this morning, he was saying "children's museum" all morning and for the whole drive to downtown (about 30 minutes). Then after we got home, he kept repeating "green roof park" over and over (for at least an hour), even though I told him repeatedly we were doing that later in the afternoon. It may not sound that bad, but trust me—when it's non-stop all day long—it begins to wear on you.

At bedtime, I was trying to persuade Justin to sleep in his "big boy bed" instead of on a pallet on the floor, and he lost it. He was screaming, "bed on floor" over and over again, interspersed with "tissue" (because he was crying and wanted a Kleenex). He kept yelling and screaming those two things over and over again, until I finally lost it and yelled at him to "stop yelling at me".

If you could see me as I'm writing this, you would see that I'm rolling my eyes at how ridiculous that must sound. That's like slapping your kid because he hit someone and then telling him that hitting is bad. I thought I did really well all day, but then to lose it like that and yell at him.... Well, I'm not very proud of myself right now. I'm continually struggling with wanting to treat Justin like a regular kid and enforce certain discipline, but I never know if he really understands things like other kids. It's so hard to figure out how tough or how soft to be sometimes.

So the regression is very noticeable, but I don't know if it's been the lack of supplements or the addition of the antibiotic that's causing his regression. Maybe it was a combination of the two. As if that wasn't enough, it's also daylight savings time, which always messes him up and makes bedtime really difficult. He had been going to bed really easily—like within 15 minutes, as opposed to the hour or two that it used to take me to put him to bed. Tonight it was back to almost an hour, and he only fell asleep out of sheer exhaustion. After he finally fell asleep, I just walked into our bedroom, shut the door, closed myself in the bathroom and sobbed for about twenty minutes.

10

Putting It All In Perspective

This is hard work. That's all there is to it. It's hard on me, it's hard on Justin, and it's hard on the rest of the family. And sometimes, just sometimes, even the strongest person will break down and cry. But after that much-needed outlet is over with, it's time to put things in perspective and focus on the good things.

At this point, I decided that every day, no matter how hard my day had been, I needed to take two minutes at the end of the day and find three things to appreciate from that day. It's always easy to focus on the bad things, but it's so much more rewarding to focus on the good. When you're constantly dealing with the stress of caring for a sick child, and trying to remember all of his supplements, and his special diet, and his doctor's appointments and the myriad of other details, it's really easy for the good stuff to happen and then quickly be forgotten.

So let's look at the positives from yesterday:

1. We didn't have any potty accidents—even with going to the park and to the Children's museum. That's a big one.

2. We had some really cute tender moments together—like watching our video clips on my video camera.

3. We had "giggle time" at the table at lunch. That was pretty hysterical. He just started giggling and then I started giggling for no reason too. That made him giggle more and so on and so forth. That's just plain good for the soul.

Our visit to the San Antonio Children's Museum was quite a revelation. What a great place for kids.... well, unless they have autism. Note to self: Don't go on the last day of Spring Break! It was overwhelming to Justin, to say the least. It was very noisy, hectic and crowded. It's a great place, though. I'm looking forward to taking Justin back when he's recovered a little bit more. We videotaped him and

I realized after watching the tape what it must be like for him every day, pretty much anywhere out in public. He looked like a deer in the headlights, like none of his filters were working and everything was just coming at him all at once—the lights, the noise, the people, everything. He was clearly overwhelmed.

03/17/2007—It's Saturday and today we began the anti-yeast medication called Diflucan. Dr. Jepson had warned me that Justin's behavior may become "very autistic" during this medication. He was right. Not only did he become very task-avoidant, argumentative and easily over-stimulated, but he started acting down-right weird, almost like he was hallucinating sometimes.

He regressed back to how he'd been before we started any of the supplements—back during the holidays in December when it was just crazy with all kinds of relatives and friends coming and going, and bedtime had become a real chore. I've been seeing such vast improvements in language and behavior for the last three months that this whole regression-thing hit me pretty hard. Once I finally got him to bed, I had another sob-session in the bathroom.

Appreciation Moments:

1. He had some moments of clarity today when he would look right at my face, touch my cheek, and say softly "Mommy, I love you."

2. We played chase and giggled for at least forty-five minutes.

3. We played a game called, "Does (insert animal here) live in the ocean?" And we traded out different animals that were obvious, like an octopus, with silly things like Winnie the Pooh.

Speech Therapy

3/20/2007—Dr. Jepson had recommended additional speech therapy for Justin, so I took him to his first speech appointment today in San Antonio. It was great to see the way his teacher worked with him. I was allowed to sit in the corner and observe quietly, which was great because I was able to pick up things to continue working on at home. I have to admit it was pretty hard to stay quiet, though. I'm so used to answering for him when someone asks him a question and doesn't get a response that it was quite a struggle to try and be invisible.

Appreciation Moments:

1. When we were at speech therapy, his teacher had shown Justin around the place—including a gym at the back of the room. This is mostly a big room used for occupational therapy with gym mats and different manipulatives. Later, she was showing Justin a picture of a kitchen with lots of different types of food on the counter. When she asked him where the jam was, he pointed to the door and said, "gym is out there". It was so cute, I couldn't help but laugh.

2. The other really cute thing was, whenever she would ask him a question, he would put his head on his hands and say "Hmm, let's see." I had never heard him make that sort of expression before, but now I've noticed that I say that a lot when I'm trying to stall—so I guess he picked that one up from me.

3. I started teaching Justin about the remote control this morning, and it was so much fun. He got such a kick out of it. In fact, he told me "Click on the arrow, Mommy" when we were playing a DVD game on Dumbo. Things are really coming together for him.

4. We went out on the front porch in the afternoon and our neighbor was out working in his yard. He came over and Justin not only said "hi", but when the neighbor asked him his name, he said clearly, "My name is Justin." Then when he asked him how old he is, Justin said, "I'm one, two, three years old" and held up his fingers. Very cool progress.

3/23/3007—Justin was insisting on playing chase over and over again today. So, I was getting tired and said—"Well let's check the clock and see what time it is." I looked at my watch and said "Yup, it says it's time for Mommy to chase you." And I got up and chased him around the kitchen.
Then we laid down and laughed and tickled and then *he said*, "Let's check the clock."
I said "What does the clock say?"
And he said "It's time for a tickle." I almost started crying, I was so happy with the interaction.

3/24/2007—Justin had a hard time waking up this morning, but once he was up, he was in a great mood. He seemed very connected and happy and answered most of my questions this morning. He's a little more clingy than usual these days and wanting me to take care of most of his needs—resisting Dave helping a little, but not too bad. He had a great morning at school, except that the kids got riled up in motor lab, all tackling each other. And when his teacher pulled Justin off another boy, Justin bit her. Not real hard, but a bite no less. She put him in time out and talked to him about it. She doesn't think it's an issue, but just wanted to mention it to me. I told her again, I think it's the anti-fungal medicine and reminded her—only two more weeks!!

Appreciation Moments:

1.   When I picked up Justin at school today, he was happy as always to see me and immediately started saying, "green roof park". I explained to him that no, we can't go to the park right now. We need to go meet Dave at the haircutting place. I told him Dave was getting a haircut and then Justin would get a haircut, to which he said "Mommy get a haircut?" I said, "No, Mommy's not getting a haircut, but you can sit in my lap to get your haircut." He said "no, no sit in lap, no haircut." I told him he's getting his picture taken tomorrow at school so we'll just get a quick haircut. I said, "Do you want to sit in Mommy's lap or the big boy chair like Dave?" He said the big chair. And that's what he did. I was actually able to reason with him!!

2.   We went to the park after his haircut and had a great time.

3.   He was very compliant with dinner, bath and bedtime tonight.

He's definitely starting to be more connected and alert again, so I'm extremely hopeful that he's getting rid of his yeast problems. He still tends to get charged up in the evening, but otherwise his behavior is getting a little bit better.

Justin's Fourth Birthday

3/29/2007—Today was Justin's birthday!! We threw Justin a little birthday party and only had a few people over for dinner, cake and presents. It was really fun and pretty low-key all and all. We had about 30 helium balloons when Justin got home from school and a bunch of presents. He did really well with all the activity and excitement—much better than expected (yea!)

Appreciation Moments:

1. Justin helped me make and decorate his birthday (GFCF) cupcakes. This was the first time he showed an interest in helping me in the kitchen.

2. He also helped me make gift bags for all of the kids in his class. They are throwing a little birthday party for him at school tomorrow.

3. Before everyone came over for dinner, Justin and I went outside on the patio and blew bubbles together. He even took turns without a fuss.

4/01/2007—Justin came back from his Dad's very happy, but soon regressed into a whiny, non-compliant child. This behavior shift seemed to coincide with feeding him a dose of the anti-yeast medication. All evening was a struggle. Playing chase, taking a bath, eating, even watching a movie became a chore and a power struggle. The only thing that surprisingly didn't suffer was his potty routine. He told me every time he needed to pee and poop.

An Epsom salt bath helped, but it was still a rough night. Justin settled down a little bit after his dinner and bath, and settled onto the couch with me to watch Ice Age: The Meltdown. Little did I realize the movie was a sign of things to come. He did not want to go to bed and had a major meltdown.

Once I finally got him in bed, I felt so sorry for him, because he could not settle his little body down. He just kept moving around and seemingly trying to get comfortable, but with little success. He acts like his skin is crawling, he's so restless. It takes a good fifteen-twenty minutes for our typical routine, but then another 15–20 minutes to settle in after that. Rubbing his forehead seems to help and eventually he finally fell asleep. I was exhausted.

Appreciation Moments:

1. It was a tough day, but at least he told me every time he needed to pee or poop.

2. Only one more week of anti-yeast medication. Yea!

3. Even though he's had some rough days at school recently, he still wants to go to school every morning. At least it's not a struggle like it used to be for the daycare.

04/02/07—Justin did not have a very good day at school. They said he was difficult all morning and only slightly better in the afternoon. He was so tired that he fell asleep on the way home. I spoke with the nurse at Thoughtful House (she was responding to a long email I sent on Friday). They moved up my follow up appointment to Friday at 2:30. We will go over all test results thus far and plan for his chelation treatment. I'm hoping we can start chelation the following weekend.

I have noticed him putting his hands in his mouth a lot and also the marbles from the Hungry Hippo game, along with his toys at bath time. Need to ask the doctor about that. Also, need to find out if Valerian root is an option for bedtime, since the melatonin did not work well for him (i.e. caused him to be more aggressive the next day).

Appreciation Moments:

1. Justin was definitely talking a lot more tonight. He's trying to make more connections and say things the right way. It's encouraging. He was still a little whiny but not nearly as bad as last night.

2. He went to sleep a little before 9:00, which was pretty good considering he slept for an hour and a half after we got home from school today. All in all it was a good night.

3. Justin kept getting down on the floor eye to eye with Bobo (our cat). He would lay down on the floor right in front of him and carry on conversations with him. It was adorable. Bobo did not seem too impressed, but was surprisingly tolerant.

04/04/2007—I started my website today (www.mothercub.com) It's a work in progress, but at least it's up and running. Justin was very intense this afternoon and all evening. It was better after he took a long Epsom salt bath. I put him to bed at 8:00, but it still took him 45 minutes to finally fall asleep.

Appreciation Moments:

1. Justin went to bed without too much of a fuss when I told him it was bedtime.

2. There were a lot of great speech things happening today. We went to pick up dinner from a local restaurant and Justin was in the back seat, saying, "Where is the restaurant?" Then later, we were talking about the

calendar and he started randomly saying he wanted today to be Tuesday because that's when we get to go to speech and see Miss Meghan (his therapist) and play in the gym and play games.

3. Watching him understand how to climb the "rock wall" part of the playground after I showed him just one time.

There are so many developmental things happening right now that are so awesome. I need to continue to focus on that. The hard part is his intensity and that whiny loud voice when he gets all fired up in the evenings. But, then when he blows me a kiss or grabs my hand or says, "Come on Mommy", all the bad stuff just seems to float away.

11

All About Yeast

Many autistic kids have issues with yeast build-up in their gastro-intestinal tracts. This condition causes many of the outward behavior issues and symptoms that are typically identified with autistic kids—the tantrums, the repetitive stimming behaviors, the aggression toward others, the frequent withdrawal from our world. It's perplexing and heart-breaking.

Dr. Stephen M. Edelson of Salem, Oregon, explains the Yeast-Autism Connection like this: "There is a great deal of evidence that a form of yeast, candida albicans, may exacerbate many behavior and health problems in autistic individuals, especially those with late-onset autism. This form of yeast is located in various parts of the body including the digestive tract. Generally speaking, benign microbes limit the amount of yeast in the intestinal tract, and thus, keep the yeast under control.

However, exposure to antibiotics, especially repeated exposure, can destroy these microbes. This can result in an overgrowth of candida albicans. When the yeast multiplies, it releases toxins in the body; and these toxins are known to impair the central nervous system and the immune system.

Some of the behavior problems which have been linked to an overgrowth of candida albicans include: confusion, hyperactivity, short attention span, lethargy, irritability, and aggression. Health problems can include: headaches, stomachaches, constipation, gas pains, fatigue, and depression. These problems are often worse during damp and/or muggy days and in moldy places."

Dr. Edelson continues by saying, "Research by Dr. William Shaw shows unusual microbial metabolites in the urine of autistic children who responded remarkably well to anti-fungal treatments. Dr. Shaw and his colleagues observed a decrease in urinary organic acids as well as decreases in hyperactivity and self-stimulatory, stereotyped behavior; and increases in eye contact, vocalization, and concentration.

There are many safe methods to treat yeast overgrowth, such as taking nutritional supplements which replenish the intestinal tract with 'good' microbes (e.g., acidophilus) and/or taking anti-fungal medications (e.g., Nystatin, Ketoconazole, Diflucan). It is also recommended that the person be placed on a special diet, low in sugar and other foods on which yeasts thrive.

Interestingly, if the candida albicans is causing health and behavior problems, a person will often become quite ill for a few days after receiving a treatment to kill the excess yeast. The yeast is destroyed and the debris is circulated through the body until it is excreted. Thus, a person who displays negative behaviors soon after receiving treatment for candida albicans (the Herxheimer reaction) is likely to have a good prognosis. If the person is suffering from autism, his/her health and behavior should improve following the therapy."5

I was beginning to feel like all of the pieces of the puzzle were coming together. We had started reinforcing Justin's immune system and overall health through nutritional supplements and GFCF diet. We had treated the bad bacteria issue in Justin's gut. We were in the process of treating the horrendous overgrowth of yeast in his entire gastro-intestinal tract. And we were addressing his speech delay through speech therapy. The next step would be checking his body for heavy metal toxicity and treating that as well.

04/06/2007—Today was a great day! I had the follow up appointment with Dr. Jepson. He told me that everything is proceeding along just fine, and I need to be patient and continue to take things one step at a time. We reviewed Justin's lab results and made a plan for the next steps of therapy.

All reports indicated that Justin's body is heavily burdened with mercury, aluminum and lead. We decided to move forward with chelation therapy and to continue increasing his nutritional supplements. We should finish the anti-yeast medication and then wait a week before doing anything else. Dr. Jepson said most of the issues I brought up (i.e. aggression, biting, dilated pupils, lack of appetite, sleep issues, adrenaline surges and general intensity) should begin to dissipate over the next week.

Anti-Yeast Meds

Since Justin's yeast reading had been off the charts, we need to add in two more supplements: Candex and Biocidin. Both should help with maintenance in keeping a healthy gut and should keep the yeast from becoming an issue again. If Justin's behavior does not improve, we may have to consider continuing anti-yeast medication or possibly taking him off the digestive enzymes.

Methyl-B12 Injections

In 7–10 days, if behavior improves, we will begin B12 shots that I will administer to him myself. Every 3 days, he will get a B12 injection—best given at bedtime, in the fat of the butt. B12 causes excitability in some children, but not for several hours. If I give it to him in the morning, it may get him amped up for nighttime, but if given to him at bedtime, it should help him wake up alert and refreshed. I'm not looking forward to that part of the treatment, but from the research I've done, the results seem to far outweigh the hassle of administering the shots.

Folinic Acid

After another week, I need to begin Folinic Acid—which is similar to folic acid, only better for autistic kids. Folinic acid is another supplement that helps the body to produce glutathione, which is typically deficient in autistic kids. After another week, I will need to add in L-glutathione transdermally (a cream on the skin). This will continue to help Justin's body to produce glutathione himself, thereby teaching his body to detoxify on its own.

We should wait another week after starting the l-glutathione cream before we begin the chelation medication. We discussed the different forms: intravenous (risky and intense), oral (goes straight to the gut and can cause recurrence of yeast and other problems), transdermal (which is questionable because you can't be sure how much is being absorbed through the skin) and finally suppositories (Dr. Jepson's recommendation because it bypasses the gut and gets absorbed right into the bloodstream through the rectum).

We agreed on the suppositories to be given once a day (after a BM or at bedtime) for three days on and 11 days off. So we will chelate every other weekend. We will follow up with the doctor in a few weeks to check and see how Justin is tolerating the chelation. Then every 3 months, we will have to do blood and urine testing to check levels of heavy metals coming out, along with blood, kidney and liver functions.

I gave Justin his bath tonight with one cup Epsom salt, and while he was in there he said, *"Mommy take a bath?"*
I said, "No, Mommy doesn't need a bath right now."
He said, "Mommy take a bath or go to bed or time away."
These are the types of choices I typically give him when I want him to choose to take a bath. This is huge progress yet again. The kid is using my love and logic on me!!

Appreciation Moments:

1. Sitting on the couch in between me and Dave, watching a movie, and having one hand on my leg and the other hand on Dave's leg. He kept stealing glances at both of us and smiling.

2. At dinner, while he was stalling eating his fish sticks, he tried using my technique of First, Then on me. He would say, "first drink, then fish sticks", and then "First potty, then movie, then fish sticks" trying to completely avoid eating all together. Pretty damn clever!! I stuck to my guns though and made him eat his fish sticks first. Score one for Mommy☺

3. While Justin was in the bath tonight, he said "Go potty" and wanted to get out of the bath to go pee in the potty. (Normally he won't tell me when he has to go—he just goes in the bath if the urge hits him while in the water.) More progress!

After his bath, he was very rough on me (physically), grabbing and hugging and tackling and climbing all over me. He was very amped up and chatty all evening, and bedtime took about an hour before he finally settled down and fell asleep. It's exhausting, but if I keep focusing on all of the good things happening, I think I can get through this.

04/10/2007—I noticed a rash pop up yesterday around his hips and some on his legs. The weather has been really cold for a few days (High 30s) and I think that's what caused it. It was worse today, so I'm not sure if I'm giving him too many Epsom baths or if it was just due to the weather change. Hopefully, the skin rash will be gone tomorrow. It had spread all over his legs, arms, sides and hips when I got him out of the bath, but I covered him in Eucerin so hopefully that will take care of it. The weather is supposed to be back up in the 80s tomorrow. Welcome to Texas!!

Appreciation Moments:

1. Teaching him how to use the remote control himself to play "What will Spot wear?" on the Discovering Spot DVD. He was pretty proud of himself whenever he did it himself.

2. Seeing his happy face when I picked him up from school.

3. When he ran off to his room and I thought he was going to slam his bedroom door, he came back and got my hand instead and walked me to his bedroom to read a book.

4. When we left the speech therapy office, he usually throws a bit of a fit because he doesn't want to go. I was expecting that, but he didn't do that this time. He listened to me and left without incident.

04/12/2007—His teacher said he had a really good day today—well, she corrected, good compared to the last 3 weeks. Also, he ate all of his lunch today!! That was huge, because for the past few months, he would only eat 1/3 or ½ of his PBJ sandwich and only some of the fruit and snacks. She did note that he has also been exceedingly thirsty.

He's been very pale lately, and yesterday he had a very scary whitish/greenish pallor to his skin. His color seemed better today. He also had a rash on his face since returning from his Dad's on Sunday. It was only on his chin at the time, but there was also food caked on his chin. When I washed his face, I noticed the small red bumps and thought they were from the food that had been on his face.

The next day, I noticed a few more small red dots on his cheeks. His cheeks seemed chapped from the cold weather over the weekend so I put Eucerin on his face and all over his body. The next day, I noticed the small red bumps on the other side of his face under his eye. Dave and I wondered if he had been given some gluten over the weekend.

Today, his color seemed so much better and the eczema on his body had gone away but it still remained on his face. We decided it's probably just a reaction from his body trying to adjust to all of the changes going on—including being off of the anti-yeast meds.

Appreciation Moments:

1. He took a nice nap after speech therapy today

2. After his bath, he hugged me tight while I was drying him off.

3. Today after bath, we traded kisses on each other's eyes, nose, mouth and he tried to kiss my teeth. It was absolutely adorable. It was his idea to trade kisses after I kissed him once on the nose.

04/13/2007—A friend of mine came over tonight with her son, who is the same age as Justin. The two boys get along fine, but Justin doesn't usually interact a whole lot. Well, tonight he did some really interesting things. For one, he mimicked everything the other little boy said or did. I had never seen him do that before. If the other boy said, "I want some milk", Justin would say, "I want some milk" (even though he doesn't drink milk). If the other boy said, "Mommy, I love you", Justin would say, "Mommy I love you." If the other boy said, "I have a cat", Justin said it too. It was really interesting to watch.

He also played much better overall. They are usually pretty hard on each other, and Justin has a tendency to tackle a lot and throw toys at him. He threw one marble at him, but once he got in trouble for that, he didn't do it anymore. They played outside on the playground set pretty well too. And when we came inside and started watching videos, Justin sat with me instead of standing in front of the television or pacing back and forth.

After they left, I gave him an Epsom salt bath tonight and also his first B12 shot. That was tough. He was scared of the needle, and now I'm being a big sissy about having to do the next one.

04/15/2007—Today was a pretty good day. We got up at 7:00, had a nice breakfast, then did our weekly grocery shopping, and then went to the park. Justin actually tried to go up and talk to a few kids. He did pretty well, but is still having a hard time getting past the initial "Hi, what's your name?" When Justin started running around with a stick, chasing some older boys, I told him no running with a stick (I sounded just like MY mother) and he threw down and had a whining fit. So I told him it was time to go. He settled down after just a few seconds and followed me out to the car. I was stunned.

04/16/2007—Justin's speech is continuing to progress, with him saying things like, "The circle goes around like this". Also, I was telling him after school that we were going to get a haircut, then go home and watch White Seal (his favorite movie of the week). And he said, "No, Mommy. First, White Seal and then haircut. That would be better, okay?" I almost drove off the road.

Then after bath time, and as I was drying him off, he grabbed a cup, put it up to his weewee and said, "go potty"—and peed in the cup. Once again, I fell on the floor laughing. Connections are being made. Enough said.

04/18/2007—Justin had a rough morning at school with non-compliance and that type of thing. I started the Biocidin today and also the Arctic Cod Liver Oil. His language continues to improve, but his behavior is still pretty inconsistent. Eye contact seems to be much better, and he's focusing a lot more on our faces. I did notice a little hand-flapping (briefly) and chewing on his inside cheek tonight, and he was a bit revved up at bedtime. I hadn't seen those things in a while, but at least they only happened briefly.

12

Sensory Integration

One of the first things our therapist with ECI told us was that she thought Justin may have something called Sensory Integration Disorder. She explained that this is a condition where the child's brain cannot properly process input from all five senses at the same time.

For most children, the senses of touch, sight, sound, movement and taste develop and work synergistically. But for a lot of autistic kids, they do not. These children tend to get easily overwhelmed whenever there is too much happening at one time. They can't process all of the incoming stimuli, so they simply withdraw into their own world where they can focus on one thing at a time.

Some of the faculty members at the University of Texas in Austin have been working together to research this condition. They have studied how this particular state affects a child's behavior, development and ability to properly interact and learn. Even better, they have created a seminar work/play day that teaches parents, educators and therapists how they can work together with their children to minimize the effects of this condition.

04/21/2007—Mom met me today at the UT Autism Project Workshop at University of Texas in Austin today. It was an interactive workshop for parents and their autistic kids, directed by two full-time faculty members of the University of Texas Kinesiology Department, Pam Buchanan and Dr. Jody Jensen.

Justin woke up with a runny nose, so I gave him a dose of Zyrtec after breakfast. Unfortunately, it made him really sleepy and whiny, but he was still excited when I told him we were "meeting Grandma at the gym to play games." I made him repeat that with me a few times to make sure he understood. By the time we got to Austin, he was saying "Where is Grandma gym?"

As soon as we arrived and filled out our paperwork, a student volunteer came up, introduced himself, and tried to take Justin off to the main gym. Mom and I were supposed to go to a classroom for a lecture, while Justin would go play games with the other kids. Justin was immediately anxious and clingy, so Mom went on to the classroom and I took Justin with the UT student into the gym.

There was a lot of cool stuff going on in there. Kids were playing with all kinds of sensory toys, jumping on trampolines, blowing bubbles and playing games. One of the directors, Pam Buchanan, came up and introduced herself and encouraged me to go off to the classroom. I didn't feel comfortable with that because we had just arrived, and I could tell Justin was a little overwhelmed. Pam reassured me that she and the students were quite experienced and I should leave Justin in their capable hands and go on to the classroom.

The lecture was very enlightening and the speaker (Jody Jensen) was amazing. She talked about how autism is primarily a sensory integration issue. She told us, "We are not here today to cure autism or to find out what caused it—other people are busy doing that. We are here to encourage you to find out what your children are sensitive to and to desensitize them through hands-on play."[6]

She explained what sensory integration disorder really means by using the analogy of it being winter time when your child's skin is already dry and itchy. Then you might dress her in a wool sweater that scratches at her neck all day. Then you expect her to ride in a cloth car seat, and then a hard vinyl bus seat, and then a really hard wooden chair at school.

These are a lot of sensory inputs that most of us can filter out, but a lot of these children simply cannot. So they might whine or throw tantrums or act out aggressively, and most of us think they are just acting up. But the bottom line is that your child is just overwhelmed and cannot filter out all of the overpowering stuff coming at her through her immature senses.

"The challenge," Jody explained, "is to identify children's unique sensory needs and to find different ways of playing with them that will make them less sensitive."[7]

One of the lecture handouts described the concept in even greater detail:

"The educational validity of play lies in the contribution of play activities to sensorimotor integration in typically and atypically developing children. The teachers, educators and the entire family can get involved in activities that have a strong focus on the sensory systems. Many childhood games and activities can be played that help facilitate this. There are many games that rely upon integration of vestibular, proprioception, auditory, visual and tactile senses. More importantly, the proper integration of these systems transfers to the successful vocational, functional living, recreational environments and independence of our children." 8

It was such a fun and informative day. After the lecture, the parents joined the kids in the gym and rotated through different stations that each had different types of games. Each station was set up to introduce the child to the different senses through play. Justin had a great time, and it was a very valuable learning experience for me and Grandma too. I'm looking forward to attending the next one, hopefully later this year.

04/27/2007—Today was a great day at school—right up to the end of the day. Justin bit another child on the finger really hard—hard enough to break the skin. They were having recess outside and both boys wanted to play with the bug catcher. When Justin didn't get it, he bit the other little boy. Then, he knew he was in trouble so he took off running—straight toward the parking lot. His teacher chased after him, yelling for him to stop because he was getting close to where a lot of cars were coming and going. He thought she was playing chase with him, so he took it into high gear and it scared the daylights out of her. Needless to say, she's requested that we not play chase games at home anymore.

05/01/2007—Dave got home from his trip while Justin and I were playing with magnets (called magnetix). Justin ran up and hugged Dave and then said, "Dave, we're playing magnets." Then he said, "Dave, do you want to play magnets with us?" It was so awesome to watch him have a spontaneous interaction (and sharing enjoyment) with DAVE!!

Daily Surprises

At dinner on Wednesday night, Dave and I were eating salad and Justin was having his gluten-free baked fish sticks, cantaloupe and blueberries. Justin said "what's that?" as I guided a forkful of spinach salad to my mouth. I told him, "It's salad, do you want to try it?" and he actually said "Yes". He wasn't expecting the slimy texture of the spinach and almost threw up when he got it in his mouth, but he managed to get it down. Needless to say, he didn't want anymore, but at least he tried it.

On Thursday night, Dave made Crispy Pork Cutlets—thinly breaded (GF/CF) pork cutlets, pounded thin. We also served corn and fruit. Justin took one look at his plate and threw a fit. He wanted a hot dog. I stood my ground and said, no, this is what we're having for dinner. He wandered around and then started saying, "backyard". I told him "first dinner, then backyard". He continued to fuss and continued wandering around the table. To our shock and surprise, when he rounded the table on about his third lap, he reached up and grabbed a bite of the pork. He chewed on it for a bit and then did a few more laps around the table. Then he came back to the table, and ate the rest of the pork and cantaloupe. We decided not to push it with the corn.

Behavior was up and down all week. I was a little disappointed because we had started giving the B12 shots every other day and I was expecting a better outcome. After a little research, I think it's because I've probably been giving the shots too deep, which forces the B12 into the muscle (instead of the fat). Apparently, when you give the shot straight in, it goes into muscle—even though it's a very small needle. This explains why his pee is red-tinged the next day. When it goes into the muscle it gets absorbed very quickly and half of it is peed out the next day. When it goes into fat, the absorption is slower and the results are better because they last for about three days, as opposed to being immediate and then going away quickly.

05/07/2007—We had another great afternoon today, and Justin had a great day at school. He ate all of his breakfast, lunch and dinner. He was mostly compliant and just very, very happy. We played games on the computer and when the computer would lock up, he said, "Watch this—the computer is thinking". Then in the bathtub later on, he stayed in there for forty minutes playing and floating and splashing around. I heard him throwing all of the toys into the tub and saying—"Look at this—what a mess!" It was glorious to hear those words!!!

He fell asleep in about twelve minutes of our bedtime routine. He was stretched out on his side, looking at my face and holding my hand. My heart runneth over …

5/08/2007—Justin's speech has been exploding! Is it from the extra speech therapy or the B12 shots or the GFCF diet or the supplements? That's the tough part—I don't know exactly what's working and what's not—so I keep doing everything. It's been about four months since we started this adventure, and this Friday will be the first round of chelation. Hopefully, we'll see another big jump this time next week.

13

Chelation Therapy

"Autism is a disease of immune dysregulation," Dr. Jepson told me at one of our first consultations. "That means the immune system is not working properly. It's a very complex issue to resolve, and several problems will need to be addressed in order to return your child's body back to any sort of normalcy. This will include working to resolve mineral and vitamin deficiencies, gastro-intestinal interventions, nutritional deficiencies, and possible chelation of heavy metal toxins."9

Chelation therapy is a process used to specifically remove mercury and other heavy metals from the body. Once the heavy metals are removed, the body has a chance to return to a normal balance and health. Neurological, behavioral and physiological symptoms typically resolve or improve after chelation therapy, which may take anywhere from twelve to twenty-four months, depending on how toxic the child is when the process begins.

According to the Generation Rescue website, "When monitored appropriately, chelation therapy to remove toxic metals from your child's body is a safe and straightforward treatment that has been used for decades to remedy many degenerative, neurological, and auto-immune disorders…. Everyday, more is being learned about mercury toxicity and its treatment—making the healing of our mercury-poisoned children even more effective and safe."10

DMSA Suppositories

05/11/07—I had to give Justin his first DMSA suppository tonight to begin his chelation treatment. It was awful. Not much fun for either one of us! He was squirming and kept saying "No, no—it hurts!" and I felt like I was violating my own son. Then realizing that I have that to look forward to every other week for at least the next year (or maybe two) was pretty depressing. But I know this is going to help him tremendously, so I need to quit being such a wimp....

05/12/2007—Justin did not go to bed until around 10:00 last night, and I was worried that he might wet the bed, but he woke up at eight this morning and had no accidents! I noticed his pee had a foul odor to it, much like his breath often smells and I wondered if there's a connection with the heavy metals and halitosis.

My best friend called today and told me her boyfriend's nephew has been diagnosed with autism. The boy's mother is devastated. Every day it's the same thing—somebody, somewhere is being affected by this epidemic.

By mid-morning, Justin had a red raised rash on his cheeks and back of his neck. Later in the day I noticed it was a brighter red and more pronounced. By late afternoon I noticed the raised bumps on his arms and legs, but by evening it seemed to diminish.

So I gave him the second dose of DMSA at bedtime. I had already given him an Aveeno bath to help soothe his skin and then dried him off and rubbed lotion on his arms and legs and just slipped the suppository in. He wasn't happy about it—again—but it was easier than last night. That was around 7:00 pm. He was very active all evening and by 8:30 the rash was back. I finally got him to bed around 9:30.

05/13/2007—Well this morning the rash was even worse. I'm worried about several things:

a. an allergic reaction to the DMSA medication

b. a rare side effect called toxic epidermal necrolysis (TEN) and closely related Stephens-Johnson's disease—starts out as a rash but can proceed to being fatal

c. an outbreak at his school of something called Fifth's Disease that presents itself—yes you guessed it—as a red rash on the face and then spreads to the body.

d. Or a possible allergic reaction to the new sunblock I had put on him on Friday since he was going to be out in the sun all day at school. I thought maybe it had gluten hidden in it and Justin was having an allergic reaction.

So I'm thinking, come on Lord, help me figure this one out a little easier!! Do I give him the third dose (Sunday night) or hold off? This is the first round and it would be nice to get him through an entire round (three doses), especially since—with the exception of the rash—he's been doing great. No vomiting, no nausea, no diarrhea, no lethargy, no seeming discomfort except for the darn rash.

I decided to wait on the third dose until I could talk to his doctor. Better safe, than sorry.

05/14/2007—The rash seemed to mostly go away last night, so I sent Justin to school. I thought it might be a rough day for him, but he ended up having the best day he's probably had all year long. What a shocker!!

05/17/2007—Unfortunately the rest of the week were probably the hardest days he's had all year. I don't get it. I spoke with his doctor (teleconference) on Tuesday afternoon and we talked for about an hour about Justin's reaction to the DMSA. He thought that Justin's reaction sounded more like contact dermatitis (sunscreen) than a reaction from the DMSA. He told me to do a test that night and put some of the sunscreen on his belly after his bath and see if he had a rash the next day. I tried it but no rash developed.

So the doctor's advice is that it may just be some ingredient in the DMSA that is causing an allergic reaction and that next time I should give him a dose of Benadryl an hour prior to the DMSA dose. The doc said he didn't feel like the reaction was either the TEN or Fifth's Disease, and that since Justin did not show any other adverse affects, he would like me to continue with the DMSA—at least for another round to see how it goes.

05/18/2007—Today was Fun Day at school, which was another day outside all day. We slathered the same sunscreen on him, and he didn't develop any kind of reaction. So I think we can now rule out him being allergic to the sunscreen. He had a fabulous day.

05/21/2007—Today was another great day. Justin received an award for "most cheerful" at the end of year awards ceremony for his class. He had a great day, and we took him to see Shrek The Third. He was really good throughout the whole movie.

05/25/2007—Justin woke up very happy again. He's just so much more connected with the world. I went in to his bedroom at 7:30 this morning and he sat up, smiled and said "good morning, Mommy". When I asked him if he needed to go potty, he grabbed my hand and I followed him to his bathroom. He pointed at the potty (seat was already up) and he said "Look". He had independently gotten up at some point in the early morning and peed by himself!

The Miracle Grandchild

05/27/2007—This was the best weekend yet with Grandma and Papa. I started the second round of chelation on Friday and found that if I give him ½ tsp Benadryl 45 minutes prior to the DMSA, he has no rash and does just fine. Also, I added a little KY jelly to the suppository and it slipped in much easier. I have to distract him and tell him "don't laugh", which immediately makes him start laughing. Then I have him count to ten while the medicine gets absorbed. That's it! He did great!!

All weekend, he interacted with me and his grandparents better than ever. His appetite was great. His mood was great. He talked to all the neighbors when we went out in the golf cart. He kept saying, "We're driving around the neighborhood." My Mom and Dad refer to him as their Miracle Grandchild, because of all the amazing progress they've seen in him over the last four or five months. We went to see the waterfall (on the golf course) which had overflowed due to all the recent rain. Justin loved it and kept asking to go back and see it again and again. Then we got out and threw small stones into the water. He almost had a fit when it was time to leave, but I distracted him and everything was just fine. He climbed back up in the golf cart and said, "Come on, Mommy. Let's go."

05/29/2007—Justin is still just as happy and connected as could be. He's sleeping well, eating well, and not nearly as interested in watching movies and videos. His new obsession is the computer. He had not shown much of an interest in the computer at all, except to sit in my lap and watch me play video games. Then it seemed like overnight he suddenly understood how to navigate through a website with the mouse. It's literally amazing.

Justin helped me set the table for dinner, clean up after dinner and make up the beds. He was very compliant and happy to help. You can just tell how much better he feels. Dad called and kept commenting on how wonderful the changes are in him and how it's like night and day since December.

14

The Journey Continues

I don't want to mislead you into thinking that I'm skipping around here like Mary Poppins all the time. It's not like I need a reality-check. Believe me, I get one of those at least once a day. I have many of my own less-than-stellar parenting days, and the biggest thing that usually gets me is the guilt.

Guilt about what, you may be wondering. Well, where there's guilt, there's usually plenty to go around. What I mean by this is, sometimes we may be having a really bad day all the way around. Justin has been running around here, yelling or stimming and really intense or moody or maybe it's been raining and he's got cabin-fever, or Dave has just returned from a trip and Justin is clinging to me not wanting to share me with anyone. Those are pretty tough days, and they happen fairly regularly—although thankfully starting to happen less and less.

Those are the guilt-ridden days. I feel like I'm not spending enough quality time with my son or my husband. I'm in a rotten mood myself and maybe my patience-switch is a little shorter than usual. I really want and crave some me-time and feel guilty about wanting and needing that. I'm flat-tired, worn-out and crabby, and I feel guilty about that. I'm really wanting and needing to do some writing, but by the time I get Justin to bed at 8:30, clean up the kitchen and get things ready for the next day, my creativity is nowhere to be found.

There's plenty of that guilt-stuff to go around and make everyone miserable. And those are the days that I really need to remember to appreciate the wondrous things that are happening on a daily basis. That's why it's so important to keep track of the good things—the things I can appreciate. On those rough and tumble days, I go back through my Appreciation Moments and get the reality check needed to keep on moving forward.

05/31/2007—Justin woke up super happy and so talkative today. He was still asleep at 7:15, so I had to wake him up. He sat up in bed, looked up at his bulletin board and said, "My papers from school". I had pinned up a few of his art projects from school a few weeks ago, and it's like he finally saw them today.

Then, he came out of his room, hugged me and Dave, and said "good morning Bobo" (to the cat). Then he looked at the couch and said, "My movies are all gone". I had put away all of his videos that he was stacking up on the couch the night before. He asked me where they were, and I told him they were in the cabinet. Then he said, "the movies are up in the cabinet". The new complexity of his language is astounding. It's like it's been in there all along and just couldn't come out. Now it's coming out every day!

At breakfast, we started playing the "ding, dong" game. I have no idea where this came from, but Justin started saying "ding, dong". Then I would say "who is it?", and he would say "It's Mommy". Then we would continue the game and cycle through everyone he knows. It was adorable and such a fun interaction.

Xango

Current research is now showing that inflammation in the body (and especially the brain) may be one of the most significant issues that autism-sufferers have to deal with. As I began reading about this part of the autism condition, it occurred to me that I already had a product in my arsenal (i.e., my refrigerator) that might be able to help Justin with this important health issue. It was like a light bulb had suddenly been turned on in my head.

I began taking a product called Xango over a year ago for myself, and I believe it has not only helped me with recurring headaches, but with other issues like dry skin, fatigue, weight control, cholesterol, and stomach issues. It's a cranberry-colored fruit juice made from a fruit called the mangosteen. The mangosteen has played a key role in ancient Southeast Asian medicine for thousands of years, due to its extremely potent antioxidant properties, but is only recently gaining its much-deserved attention in the United States. For more information on Xango, go to: http://www.mymangosteen.com/sperry.

I had never even considered giving it to Justin, but as the light bulb grew brighter in my brain, I realized that if it could help fight infection, fatigue, bacteria, allergies, diarrhea, eczema, digestion issues, and dehydration in adults, it just might benefit my sick child too. After all, these conditions are prevalent in most autistic kids and Justin had certainly exhibited all of these problems at one time or another. In addition, I was already well-aware of the fact that Xango is an excellent antioxidant and anti-inflammatory agent. All of this—and Justin even likes the taste of it!

I began supplementing Justin with an ounce of Xango in the mornings and evenings. He immediately starting sleeping better, his color and appetite improved, and he continued to show more interest in the people and world around him.

06/07/07—Justin's language continues to improve. This morning, I asked him "Justin, how old are you?" And he said clearly, "I'm four years old—just had a birthday." I almost started crying; I was so happy to hear his answer in a full sentence.

At speech therapy this week, the therapist did something really cool. First, she showed Justin a picture of a man and a cow. Then she read a simple, four-sentence story that went like this: *The farmer's name is Joe. Joe has a cow with spots. The cow gives Joe milk. Joe likes his cow.*

Next, she asked Justin the following questions: *1. What is the farmer's name? 2. What does the farmer have? 3. What does the cow do?* And Justin would repeat the question and then answer it. It was awesome!! Sometimes he tries to avoid the work because it's hard for him. He tries to distract her by grabbing at things or getting up to look at something else in the room, but she just redirects him right back to her question and makes him sit down, focus and try his best to answer it.

06/08/2007—The supplementation schedule is getting pretty heavy and complicated at this point. Every day has to be planned out, since his supplements are to be given at certain times and with certain types of food. There is not much spontaneity in our lives at the moment, but I'll trade spontaneity for my son's health any day of the week! Here's what the typical daily schedule looks like:

- ½ cup diluted organic pear juice in the morning with colostrum, liquid vitamin mineral blend, along with DMG tablet dissolved in hot water with magnesium

- ¼ cup applesauce with fish oil, calcium, digestive enzyme, Biocidin, GABA and 5HTP

- GFCF breakfast with protein, carb & fruit, along with one ounce of Xango juice and two JuicePlus+ gummies

- Digestive enzyme in ¼ cup applesauce with GFCF lunch, plus water

- Afternoon—drink mixture again with only vitamin/mineral supplement, plus chips and hummus or fruit smoothie (mixed with 5HTP and probiotic supplements)

- Dinner—drink mixture with vitamin, mineral and colostrum supplements

- ¼ cup applesauce with fish oil, cod liver oil (for Vitamin A), calcium, digestive enzyme, Biocidin, zinc, folacal, taurine, GABA and selenium supplements

- GFCF dinner and JuicePlus+ gummies, along with one ounce of Xango juice

- 1 cup Epsom salt in bath, along with ½ cup Baking soda. After bath, 1 ml L-glutathione cream rubbed on his stomach or his back (he gets to choose).

- Every 3 days I give him his B12 shot. To do this, I put him to bed, wait 30 minutes, go in and rub numbing lidocaine cream on one of his hind cheeks, wait another 30 minutes and then give him the B12 shot in his rear end. The trick is always trying to remember which cheek I put the numbing cream on.

- Every other weekend, I give him a DMSA suppository for three nights for heavy metal detoxification chelation. To do this, I put a little lubricant on a suppository and insert right after his bath and hold it in for 10–15 seconds for it to dissolve. I have to tell him "don't laugh" and then he starts laughing and it's over. I also make him count to ten with me in Spanish to distract him while it dissolves.

I explain all of this, not to pat myself on the back, but to prepare you ahead of time for what may be required of you. I don't want to sugar-coat it. There's no doubt that this is a lot of stuff to remember and a lot of stuff to do. It can be very overwhelming on some days, but I just try to do the best I can and know that it's better than doing nothing at all.

And, most importantly, when you compare doing all of this to what otherwise may be a lifetime of family and financial strife, this is nothing. And the results are phenomenal. At least they have been for Justin. And they just might be for your child too.

In Summary

On the tough days (which seem to be about every couple of days) I have to constantly remind myself that this is not forever. It's an investment right now in my son's health and my son's future, along with the future happiness of our entire family. I have to remind myself that by next summer, Justin will be just like all the other little kids out there—only healthier.☺

I have high hopes for that. I can now finally envision trips to the zoo and the park and the amusement parks and little league and swimming and museums, whereas only six months ago, I had pretty much resigned myself to the fact that we would have a very different life than the one I had imagined when I was pregnant with Justin.

Now I can see that the life I originally imagined for my son is well within my reach. He's learning every day. His social skills are expanding. His language is on track and I think by the end of the year, he'll be close to catching up with his peers.

His overall health has improved dramatically. His horizons are broadening every day. His demeanor and interaction with people is much-improved. His incredible brain is opening up now that we're starting to get all of the junk out of his body.

Today, I'm happy to say, we have a little boy who is well on the road to recovery. We're not there yet, but we're definitely on our way. We were given a priceless gift that day in Dallas when we were told about Generation Rescue; a gift that can never be repaid, except to share the information with others and to appreciate every single day.

Every single day, we've learned to rejoice in even the smallest accomplishments, because they are, in essence, incredible victories. Every single day, we are reminded of how precious a new word, a simple understanding or a loving action can be. Every single day, we realize how truly blessed and lucky we are.

We are living examples of what can be done if you're willing to make the commitment and go the extra mile for your child. We are well on our way, folks. Kindergarten—here we come!!

REFERENCES

1. Blaylock Wellness Report, Dr. Russell Blaylock, Vol. 3, No. 8, August, 2006

2. Blaylock Wellness Report, Dr. Russell Blaylock, Vol. 1, No. 1, May, 2004

3. Mercury, Lead, and Zinc in Baby Teeth of Children With Autism Versus Controls, by Adams JB, Romdalvid J, Ramanujam VM, Legator MS

4. Autism Research to Continue with Increased Federal Funding, article on website (http://www.ed.psu.edu/news/autism.asp), speech given by Duane F. Alexander, Director of NICHD

5. The Candida Yeast-Autism Connection, Stephen M. Edelson, Ph.D., Center for the Study of Autism, Salem, Oregon

6. Dr. Jody Jensen, quoted from speech given at University of Texas Autism Project Workshop, April, 2007

7. Dr. Jody Jensen, quoted from speech given at University of Texas Autism Project Workshop, April, 2007

8. Quoted from lecture handout at University of Texas Autism Project Workshop, April, 2007

9. Dr. Bryan Jepson, quoted from personal telephone consult on May 15, 2007

10. Generation Rescue website (http://www.generationrescue.org)

The Mother Cub Autism Resource Guide

Recommended Reading:

- *Changing the Course of Autism*, Dr. Bryan Jepson
- *Children With Starving Brains*, Dr. Jacqueline McCandless
- *Evidence of Harm*, David Kirby
- *Special Diets for Special Kids*, Lisa Lewis, Ph.D.
- *Love & Logic: Magic for Early Childhood*, Jim Fay & Charles Fay, Ph.D.

Organizations/Websites:

- Generation Rescue—www.generationrescue.org
- Autism Research Institute—www.autism.com
- Thoughtful House for Children—www.thoughtfulhouse.org
- National Vaccine Information Center—www.nvic.org
- Autism Education Network—www.autismeducation.net

Supplements:

- Kirkman Nutritional Supplements—www.kirkmanlabs.com
- BrainChild Nutritionals—www.brainchildnutritionals.com
- JuicePlus+ Products—www.lornaenglemanmd.com
- Omega-Cure Fish Oil—www.omegacure.com
- Even Better Now—www.evenbetternow.com

Newsletters/Publications:

- Schafer Autism Report—www.sarnet.org
- Blaylock Wellness Guide, by Dr. Russell Blaylock—www.blaylockreport.com
- Autism Info—www.autisminfo.com
- Talk About Curing Autism—www.tacanow.com
- M.I.N.D. Institute—www.ucdmc.ucdavis.edu/mindinstitute/newsroom/newsletter

Other Helpful Products

- ANDI Protein Bars—www.autismndi.com
- Xango Juice—www.mymangosteen.com/sperry
- Digestive Enzymes—www.houstonzymes.com
- Byonetics—www.byonetics.org
- Wheatgrass Juice—www.dynamicgreens.com

978-0-595-47918-4
0-595-47918-9

www.ingramcontent.com/pod-product-compliance
Lightning Source LLC
Chambersburg PA
CBHW051254050326
40689CB00007B/1198